THE LITTLE BOOK OF

RESTORATIVE JUSTICE IN EDUCATION

Published titles include:

The Little Book of Restorative Justice: Revised & Updated,
by Howard Zehr

The Little Book of Conflict Transformation, by John Paul Lederach

The Little Book of Family Group Conferences, New-Zealand Style, by Allan
MacRae and Howard Zehr

The Little Book of Strategic Peacebuilding, by Lisa Schirch

The Little Book of Strategic Negotiation,
by Jayne Seminare Docherty

The Little Book of Circle Processes, by Kay Pranis

The Little Book of Contemplative Photography, by Howard Zehr

The Little Book of Restorative Discipline for Schools, by Lorraine Stutzman
Amstutz and Judy H. Mullet

The Little Book of Trauma Healing, by Carolyn Yoder

The Little Book of Biblical Justice, by Chris Marshall

The Little Book of Restorative Justice for People in Prison,
by Barb Toews

The Little Book of Cool Tools for Hot Topics,
by Ron Kraybill and Evelyn Wright

El Pequeño Libro de Justicia Restaurativa, by Howard Zehr

The Little Book of Dialogue for Difficult Subjects,
by Lisa Schirch and David Campt

The Little Book of Victim Offender Conferencing,
by Lorraine Stutzman Amstutz

The Little Book of Restorative Justice for Colleges and Universities, by David R.
Karp

The Little Book of Restorative Justice for Sexual Abuse, by Judah Oudshoorn with
Michelle Jackett and Lorraine Stutzman Amstutz

*The Big Book of Restorative Justice: Four Classic Justice & Peacebuilding Books
in One Volume,* by Howard Zehr, Lorraine Stutzman Amstutz, Allan MacRae, and
Kay Pranis

The Little Book of Transformative Community Conferencing,
by David Anderson Hooker

The Little Book of Restorative Justice in Education,
by Katherine Evans and Dorothy Vaandering

The Little Book of Restorative Justice for Older Adults,
by Julie Friesen and Wendy Meek

The Little Book of Race and Restorative Justice, by Fania E. Davis

The Little Book of Racial Healing,
by Thomas Norman DeWolf, Jodie Geddes

The Little Book of Restorative Teaching Tools,
by Lindsey Pointer, Kathleen McGoey, and Haley Farrar

The Little Book of Police Youth Dialogue
by Dr. Micah E. Johnson and Jeffrey Weisberg

The Little Book of Youth Engagement in Restorative Justice
by Evelín Aquino, Anita Wadhwa, and Heather Bligh Manchester

The Little Books of Justice & Peacebuilding present, in highly
accessible form, key concepts and practices from the fields of
restorative justice, conflict transformation, and peacebuilding. Written
by leaders in these fields, they are designed for practitioners, students,
and anyone interested in justice, peace, and conflict resolution.

The Little Books of Justice & Peacebuilding series is a cooperative
effort between the Center for Justice and Peacebuilding of Eastern
Mennonite University and publisher Good Books.

THE LITTLE BOOK OF
RESTORATIVE JUSTICE IN EDUCATION

Fostering Responsibility, Healing, and Hope in Schools
REVISED & UPDATED

KATHERINE EVANS and DOROTHY VAANDERING

New York, New York

Good Books books may be purchased in bulk at special discounts for sales promotion, corporate gifts, fund-raising, or educational purposes. Special editions can also be created to specifications. For details, contact the Special Sales Department, Good Books, 207 West 36th Street, 11th Floor, New York, NY 10018 or info@skyhorsepublishing.com.

Good Books is an imprint of Skyhorse Publishing, Inc.®, a Delaware corporation.

Visit our website at www.goodbooks.com

10 9 8 7 6 5 4

Library of Congress Cataloging-in-Publication Data is available on file.

Print ISBN: 978-1-68099-859-7
eBook ISBN: 978-1-68099-865-8

Printed in the United States of America

Contents

Preface

The Little Book of Restorative Justice in Education (LB of RJE) arrived in 2016, affirming and building on the content of two earlier Little Books, *The Little Book of Circle Processes* by Kay Pranis (2005) and *The Little Book of Restorative Discipline for Schools* by Lorraine Stutzman Amstutz and Judy Mullet (2005). In the field of education at that time, ten years of engagement with restorative justice (rj) principles and practices by educators who were eager to create healthier school communities had shown that rj had potential as a practice, but that it required a concise, clear articulation of theory. Such a framing would better support effective implementation and help to explain what occurred when efforts to implement rj were unsuccessful.

The LB of RJE (2016) conveyed the insights gleaned by various educators and education researchers, and, in the six years it has been available, its content has served the purpose of contributing to a significantly deeper understanding of restorative justice in education (rje).[1] At the time of its writing, as authors, we could not have imagined what the next years would bring. Unrest at every level of society, combined with several years of pandemic life, caused us to reflect again and again on our recommendations in that small volume. Though we were concerned that our insights might not actually stand up to the challenges schools were confronting, we are grateful to hear repeatedly that educators and community youth leaders, many of whom are facing or attempting to address discrimination and oppression of all kinds, are finding support and insight in the pages we had written. This response has been humbling, for we know that we were only able to share what we did at that time because of what we had learned from others and what our own life experiences had taught us.

As rje has continued to grow and expand, our learning and our experiences have also grown and expanded. Globally, engagement with rje is now common, and few educators would say they have not heard of it. Significant research has been conducted, better identifying the progress and pitfalls of various efforts.[2] And ultimately, the collaborative conversations that have come about because of the LB of RJE are numerous, deepening insights that are waking us up to what we have yet to learn. As such, it is time for a revision of the 2016 edition.

As in the 2016 edition, we continue to identify that the purpose of the book is to serve as a reference point:

> Like a compass whose needle points us toward our destination, theory guides our practice.[3] A reference point that practitioners can return to when the daily challenges of school arise is necessary to ensure clarity and consistency.

Without it, there is a strong temptation to revert to the punitive, rewards-based approaches that school systems have unsuccessfully relied on. *The Little Book of Restorative Justice in Education* serves as [one potential] compass needle.

What we have changed has come about because we, as authors, continued to apply the core concepts in the LB of RJE to our own lives, which led to the work of interrogating our whiteness, our adultness, and our privilege. Through the patience, grace, and challenges gifted to us by many rje advocates who are Indigenous, Black, People of Color, and/or youth, and who continue to bear the burden in a society rife with oppression, we recognize that this edition must point to and promote their leadership in the field. We are excited that this is recognized by Good Books itself in its recent publications of *The Little Book of Race and Restorative Justice, The Little Book of Racial Healing,* and *The Little Book of Youth Engagement and Restorative Justice,* as each highlights what needs to be at the core of rje—the voices and the humanity of those who have traditionally been silenced.

In 2016, we were conscious of and acknowledged our indebtedness to Indigenous, Black, and People of Color for their resilience in keeping these ways of being alive through generations of genocide. In 2022, we do our best to magnify and amplify these leaders who have mentored and shown us that if rje is to thrive in schools today, those of us in dominant positions must learn to step back, listen deeply, follow their lead, and create spaces for authentically working together.

From the 2016 edition, we maintained the three interconnected components; however, we have included more discussion about the necessity for community connectedness. One of our learnings over the past six years is that work done in isolation will be less effective than work done collaboratively. Connecting with families, faith communities, and community organizations can provide opportunities to understand the complexities of relationships, deepen our understanding about harms, needs, and obligations, and more fully support justice and equity initiatives. Individuals, classrooms, and even schools do not exist in a vacuum; they influence and are influenced by neighborhoods, local municipalities, and state/provincial and national dynamics. If we ignore the broader context, we will miss important connections that can help us nurture more restorative communities. Additionally, the pandemic has illuminated the reality that schools often feel overwhelmed by the needs that present themselves and are usually under-resourced to meet those needs. Connecting with resources beyond the school can provide a support for educators who are feeling overwhelmed by the unrealistic expectations placed on them.

Additionally, this 2022 edition highlights even more the significance of promoting diversity and equity in our rje initiatives. While the 2016 edition centers justice and equity as one of the three components of rje, we have learned in the past six years that simply naming a priority of promoting justice and equity does not ensure that specific actions are taken to address justice and equity. If rje is to contribute to healing and transformation, prioritizing diversity and equity cannot be an incidental part of our work. It has to be intentional. This means that as white authors, it is important to us that we center the rje work of those who have often been silenced or marginalized, including those who are Black, Indigenous, or People of Color. As one way to do that, we have added acknowledgments at the beginning of this book of people who have had an impact on our own thinking since the 2016 edition as well as footnotes and references to their work throughout. We feel strongly that the LB of RJE is only complete when read in conjunction with those resources so we can truly learn from those whose history, culture, race, and language have allowed for the field of rj and rje to develop.

In this edition, we continue to uphold that restorative justice implemented in educational environments is grounded in key beliefs that all people are worthy and interconnected and nurtured through adherence to values of respect, dignity, and mutual concern. Rje is primarily about nurturing relational, interconnected school cultures so that when harm occurs, the community can support and provide expectations for those directly and indirectly involved (Chapters 1 and 3). We continue to endorse the use of the phrase *restorative justice in education* as a framework, and the three major interconnected and equally important concepts:

- *Creating just and equitable learning environments*
- *Nurturing healthy relationships*
- *Repairing harm and transforming conflict*

However, with thanks to recommendations from Skye Bowen,[4] we highlight the role of community connections in each, recognizing there is often a disconnection between schools and their local community that hinders the implementation of rje.

We significantly revised A Brief History of RJE (Chapter 2) and now call it An *Important* History of RJE, within which we point to the Indigenous and Afro-Indigenous roots that rje relies on. We are grateful for Fania Davis, Edward Valandra, and the authors of *Colorizing Restorative Justice*[5] for authoring texts that help us to continue to learn about our history.

While we continue to use stories, examples, and brief exercises to demonstrate how these concepts can be practiced, we have updated those stories to reflect a deepening understanding of racial justice, systemic oppression, trauma and resilience, and holistic/comprehensive approaches to rje.

As authors, we are grateful for the opportunity to be involved in this work with each of you. We trust that together we can better accept the invitation that Lilla Watson, Gangulu artist, activist, educator, and academic, and her colleagues extend to us:

> If you have come here to help me, you are wasting your time. But if you have come because your liberation is bound up with mine, then let us work together.[6]

Acknowledgments

In the 2016 edition of the LB of RJE, we wrote the following acknowledgment:

> The content of this book is not our own. There are many who have informed our understanding and practice of restorative justice in education and brought us to this point of authoring this book. In particular, we are indebted to the humility and grace offered by Indigenous peoples across North America who have kept the wonder of circle dialogue alive through generations while threatened with genocide. We trust that this Little Book honors Indigenous teachers and traditions and further opens our hearts—settler-Canadians and settler-Americans—to be still and learn more fully from their wisdom so generously offered.

We continue to humbly acknowledge the wisdom of Indigenous teachers who have so generously shared the wisdom of Circles and a restorative ethos.

In the past six years, as our understanding of the history of rj has deepened, we want to do better at acknowledging the wisdom and generosity of rj practitioners and scholars of color. So, in this 2022 edition, we wish to also recognize the following authors whose lives and work have influenced us and taught us so much:

Skye Bowen (MEd) has engaged intensively with the concepts in this book in her roles as an educator, administrator, parent to three young men, and spouse to her partner, who experienced the reality of police brutality. She lives as an active member of a community in Southwestern Ontario that has struggled greatly with human rights abuses in the contexts of education, community, and the judicial system. Her insights regarding the revisions of this book are invaluable as she has both applauded our original work and challenged us to recognize more fully the roots of restorative justice that led to the significance of connection to community. She is an educator passionate about restorative justice and community and its intersection with Black Lives Matter. She is an advocate for dismantling the school-to-prison pipeline. Watch for her newly published work in the near future and check out her videos and podcasts, which are readily available online as a companion to this chapter and book.[1]

Fania Davis (PhD) has been a longtime leader in the field of rje; her work with Restorative Justice for Oakland Youth (RJOY) has informed much of our thinking about rje both in the 2016 edition and since. Her recent publication, *The Little Book of Race and Restorative Justice*,[2] has had a significant impact on this edition, deepening our understanding of the history of rj and rje (see Chapter 2) and pushing us to more clearly articulate the distinctions between interpersonal, institutional, and structural racism and oppression. In Chapter 4, we made revisions based on our growing commitment to communicate a more holistic understanding of justice and equity. It is insufficient for us to challenge interpersonal expressions of injustice in schools without also addressing places where policies and practices are perpetuating injustice and where worldviews and social norms make possible the replication of systems of oppression.

Edward Valandra (PhD), editor of *Colorizing Restorative Justice (CRJ)*[3] and senior editor at Living Justice Press, has had and continues to play a critical role in the field of restorative justice, calling for white and non-Indigenous rj practitioners to acknowledge and repair the harm caused by colonization. In Chapter 18 of *CRJ*, Valandra discusses this history and issues a clarion call for honest truth-telling, integrity, accountability, and healing. We are indebted to Dr. Valandra for much of the information in the revisions to Chapter 2 of the LB of RJE and acknowledge that we have much to still learn about the history of colonization and about how that continues to impact our educational contexts.

We also acknowledge the contribution of the **20 additional authors** in *Colorizing Restorative Justice*. Each has courageously challenged the field to rethink its current assumptions and practices. Collectively, the entire volume speaks clearly to the shortcomings of restorative justice in its early and continual iterations in westernized contexts.

Anita Wadhwa (EdD) is a teacher, restorative justice coordinator, and education sociologist. She has contributed to our learning in so many ways over the years, always challenging us to consider carefully how and if the manner in which we think of and practice restorative justice is truly equitable. Our combined insights for integrating critical pedagogy and theory with rje propels the work of rje into transformative learning and living for adults, children, and youth alike. The *Little Book of Youth Engagement in Restorative Justice* (2021),[4] which she coauthored with Evelin Aquino and Heather Bligh Manchester, illustrates her commitment to being a champion for youth empowerment. She models constantly how to let go of adult control so that youth can fully engage and become leaders in the implementation of restorative justice education in schools, community, and society.

Maisha Winn (PhD) engages with the work of theory and rje, grappling to develop educational frameworks that are transformative for educators, students, their families, and their communities. In her role as a Black researcher, educator, and parent she has developed a theoretical framework that challenges those engaged in the field of rje to consider how history, race, culture, language, and futures matter and are foundational to addressing the realities of institutional racism and racist policies that perpetuate harm for all. We highly recommend connecting her concepts as presented in her book *Justice on Both Sides*[5] to deepen the ideas in this book. Her subsequent books delve into restorative justice as pedagogical practices, considering the ways in which a commitment to restorative justice might impact the way we develop curriculum and instruction. The first, coauthored with Hannah Graham and Rita Renjitham Alfred, specifically considers Restorative Justice in the English Language Arts Classroom, while the second, a coedited volume with Lawrence T. Winn, features practitioners and scholars who articulate what rje looks like in their schools and classrooms.

Additionally, each of us would like to express gratitude to the countless educators, community leaders, family members, and students with whom we are privileged to interact on a daily basis. Their questions, creative ideas, and challenges and critiques help us to think more deeply about rje and how to live out these principles and values in our own work.

SECTION 1
Preparing for Sustainable Growth

Restorative justice in education (rje) has had a relatively short history through which various principles and practices have emerged. In Section 1, we carefully outline an overview of rje (Chapter 1), its growth over time (Chapter 2), and the beliefs and values that support sustainable implementation in educational settings (Chapter 3). We liken the growth of rje to that of a plant. This analogy is introduced as a way to illustrate the intricate (and beautiful!) process of organic growth. We trust the comparison will help explain concepts that are often overlooked—much like an established, growing root system that lies below the surface, allowing us to enjoy the beauty of a tree or other plant.

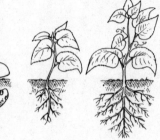

1

Chapter 1:
The Way We Do Things

Restorative justice in education (rje) is alive in story.

1. The stuffed bear is passed around a circle of twenty-one fourth-grade students. It comes to Joey, a student with communication challenges, who holds it in silence. After several moments, a few peers encourage him to speak or pass it on. The teacher stops them and reminds the group that holding the talking piece in silence is a way of communicating. Joey smiles appreciatively and then passes the bear. In the next round, two of the other students hold the bear in silence. Joey relaxes his tensed shoulders.

2. It's April, and Mr. Miller notices that his new student, Ahmed, has become withdrawn and disengaged. During their weekly Circle check-in, several students talk excitedly about the upcoming Easter break, but Ahmed passes without speaking. Later in the day, Ahmed shares with Mr. Miller that his Muslim family doesn't celebrate Easter,

but that Ramadan is about to begin. Mr. Miller apologizes for not being sensitive to Ahmed's religious traditions and later contacts a local mosque to learn more about how he can support Ahmed and other Muslim students during Ramadan.

3. The group of students approaches Ms. Gonzales, confused about the final assignment. They have worked hard yet made little progress. She is tempted to explain for the fourth time what is expected. She stops instead to listen as they respond to her questions: What is happening? What are you thinking/feeling about the work? What is the hardest thing for each of you? What impact is this having on you? What do you need from me to move forward?

4. The two ninth-grade girls, once friends, have been quarreling for days. Today, the guidance counselor takes them aside and creates a safe space for them to talk. Responding to guiding questions, the girls explain their experience, their thoughts and feelings, and the impact their situation is causing. They then thoughtfully identify what they need, and what they can offer, to move forward.

The outcome of each of these stories is like a flowering plant. Looking closely at flowers, we see beauty and complexity, a completeness that makes us wonder at their intricacy. In awe of the blooms, we rarely consider the seed that started off in darkness, or the roots under the soil supporting and feeding the plant. When we cut off the flower and put it in water, we know we can enjoy it for a few days; however, without the roots, it cannot complete its bloom and set seed for another flower.

The Purpose of This Book

The purpose of this Little Book is to direct attention to the seed, the root structure, and the supporting branches holding up the positive experiences arising from the implementation of rje. With a strong understanding of its theory and philosophy, the practice of rje can be further nurtured and strengthened. Also, when at times it fails to thrive, we may be able to identify the reason this failure happened.

The opening stories reflect the interconnected components of rje that have grown up over years of practice in schools:

- *Creating just and equitable learning environments*
- *Nurturing healthy relationships*
- *Repairing harm and transforming conflict*

These components have grown from core beliefs (seeds) that *people are worthy and relational* and are rooted in values of *respect, dignity,* and *mutual concern.*

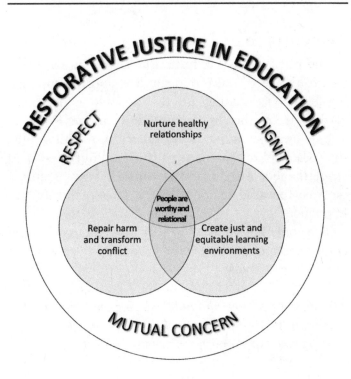

RESTORATIVE JUSTICE IN EDUCATION

RESPECT

DIGNITY

Nurture healthy
relationships

People are
worthy and
relational

Repair harm
and transform
conflict

Create just and
equitable learning
environments

MUTUAL CONCERN

Figure 1.1

As educators have engaged with rje in their various contexts, the hope they experience from it is often intertwined with questions, concerns, and misunderstandings. In this book we endeavor to build on the early, current, and growing literature available for educators to nurture the ever-expanding potential of rje. As teacher educators, we offer our insights from extensive classroom and research experience, as well as our personal commitment to the essence of restorative justice (rj) that has grown over the years. We see great benefit in connecting rje to teaching and learning theory, as well as to school climate and culture. When placed carefully and purposefully in

6

these educational contexts, the roots of restorative justice grow deeper and stronger.

What Is RJE?

Early forms of restorative justice in education borrowed from judicial settings. As a result, schools often adopted restorative justice similarly as a strategy to address behavioral issues, resolve conflict, and address harm. However, when restorative justice circle conferencing was employed in schools and facilitated with care and consistency, the significance of interconnected relationships became evident. Repairing harms required more than involving those directly affected by an incident. Rj became a shared responsibility, a commitment to creating just and equitable learning environments. In these holistic responses, rje advocates were challenged first to rethink their assumptions about *justice*, *restorative*, and *education*, and then to consider how rj was being implemented in the institutional structure of a school. (See Chapter 2 for details regarding the history of rje.)

Definitions

Restorative justice in education encompasses a variety of terms and approaches. Some of the most common include restorative practices, restorative discipline, restorative approaches, restorative measures, and restorative justice practices. Alongside these, forms of peer mediation, trauma-informed practices, social-emotional learning (SEL), peacebuilding, and antibullying programs also share some goals of rje for improving school climate, safety, and learning. How do we understand these

7

overlapping approaches, and how might rje bring together the strongest elements of each?

The phrase *restorative justice in education* synthesizes and amplifies what is shared among the perspectives, pointing us in a clearer direction. In this book, the terms *justice, restorative,* and *education* are defined as follows:

Justice honors the inherent worth and interconnectedness of all. It is enacted through relationships, through community. Primary justice, sometimes called social justice, is the condition of respect, dignity, and the protection of rights and opportunities for all, existing in relationships where no one is wronged. Secondary justice, sometimes called judicial justice, is understood mainly as a response to harm or crime.[1] In the context of this book, primary justice *nurtures* worth and interconnectedness and secondary justice *reestablishes* worth and interconnectedness

RESTORATIVE JUSTICE

Figure 1.2

Restorative, as an adjective for both primary and secondary justice, describes how an individual's or group's dignity, worth, and interconnectedness will be nurtured, protected, or reestablished, to the extent possible, in ways that will allow people to be fully contributing members of their communities.

Education comes from the Latin word *educare,* meaning "to lead out, to draw out." Therefore, it includes learning in all contexts, formal and informal, and seeks to empower learners of all ages to live out their capacity for being human and relational.

Each of these words on its own presumes and reflects a view of human beings as unique and full of potential. When its elements are combined, the term *restorative justice in education* can be defined as

> *facilitating learning communities that nurture the capacity of people to engage with one another and their environment in a manner that supports and respects the inherent dignity and worth of all.*

Ultimately rje is a vision of education that acknowledges that our individual and collective well-being is enhanced less through personal striving than through collective engagement and support.

RJE: The Way We Do Things Around Here

When restorative justice is understood holistically, it intersects with educational institutions from preschool to university in ways that stimulate cultural norms—"the way we do things around here."

It is important to recognize that the *culture* of a school grows out of people's beliefs and values. In the busyness of life and learning, these are often assumed, rarely discussed, and regularly misunderstood. Implementing rje is most successful when time is taken to identify and commit to certain core beliefs and values. What are these core beliefs and values?

Returning to the diagram (Figure 1.1), we can see these more clearly. The *core beliefs* of rje are that all human beings are worthy and interconnected. Rje recognizes people's need to belong or the "universal human wish to be connected to others in a good way."[2] These beliefs are supported by three key *values*: respect, dignity, and mutual concern. Within these values, a variety of others can also be identified based on the differing needs of people. For example, suppose that to be at your best when you are with others, *trust, honesty,* and *encouragement* are three things you value. However, a peer may identify that *responsibility, promptness,* and *humor* are key values required for the peer to feel worthy and interconnected. What is important for our discussion of rje is that

- beliefs and values nurture the well-being of self and others, and
- well-being involves the whole of the educational experience.

Chapter 3 discusses the underlying beliefs and core values of rje in more detail. Chapters 4–6 discuss the following three necessary components of restorative school cultures.

10

- *Creating just and equitable learning environments*
- *Nurturing healthy relationships*
- *Repairing harm and transforming conflict*

Creating just and equitable learning environments means that all students and staff will be acknowledged and accepted for who they are, including their race, gender, sexuality, socioeconomic status, religion, language, etc. Everyone should have the opportunity to participate in providing and receiving resources and support for their own and others' learning experiences so that they can each experience life to its fullest extent.

Ultimately, the purpose of rje is to create spaces of belonging that embrace everyone in the ways they require. This involves the use of culturally responsive pedagogy and curriculum, diverse instructional approaches, social-emotional learning, an attention to trauma and resilience, explicit ongoing engagement with human rights concepts in all curriculum, and social interaction that embodies justice and equity *not* as equal distribution of resources but as the respectful meeting of needs.

Nurturing healthy relationships acknowledges that social and emotional health are critical for learning and living. Students and educators alike thrive when they feel accepted and respected by those nearby. Thus respect, inclusion, conflict resolution, reciprocal learning and teaching, decision-making, etc., are integrated within all aspects of education—i.e., curriculum, pedagogy, hallway interactions, lunchroom and bus environments, administrative and policy

11

protocol, staff meetings, family-school engagement, and school-community partnerships.

Repairing harm and transforming conflict acknowledges that conflict and harm are a normal part of life and often provide opportunities for learning and transformation. Together, all involved in the community learn to communicate clearly in order to identify harms, to encourage accountability for those who have caused harm, and to accept and address the needs of those harmed and those causing harm. To be sustainable, rje must be understood holistically. Without explicit engagement with core beliefs and values, there will be no reference point to return to when the way becomes unclear or confused.

Inherent in all three of these components is the need for strong partnerships within and between members of the school community and the local community, where all entities understand their interconnectedness. The following image illustrates the ways in which rje takes an ecological approach to relationally based collaboration.

A comprehensive approach to rje means that we develop practices in all three of the overlapping components (Figure 1.1) and emphasize working in partnership with all of those connected to the school (Figure 1.3). One mis-implementation of rje that we have seen is an overemphasis on one of the components without working at the others.

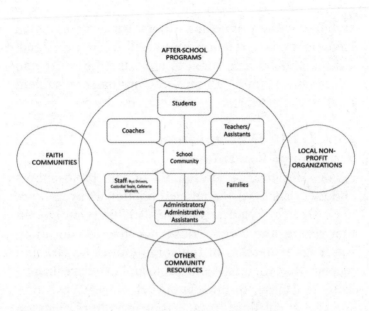

Figure 1.3

If a school chooses to focus only on restorative justice as a practice to address incidents of harm while ignoring the learning environment and the nurturing of healthy relationships, it is possible that agreements reached for addressing harm (usually an outcome of rj practices) will not be sustainable and may actually cause further harm. If the focus is on nurturing and maintaining healthy relationships and encouraging interconnected classrooms and school communities, but responses to inappropriate behavior are primarily punitive and rewards-driven, students will experience a double standard that undermines their sense of worth and well-being. In the same way, if emphasis is given to creating just and equitable learning environments, but the curriculum ignores the race or religion of some students while privileging others, trust—an essential element of just relationships—will be undermined. Ultimately, a commitment to honoring the worth and interconnectedness of human beings must be evident in all areas of education and community.

How Is RJE Different from Traditional Education?

For decades, many educational philosophers and theorists have encouraged relational engagement (e.g., Dewey, Vygotsky, Freire, Noddings, Kohn). In that regard, the core of rje is not new to education. Rje is an expression of the communities of care and respect that theorists and philosophers have historically encouraged in schools. However, new perspectives take time to take root in culture. Though education provides significant hope, it also serves as a means for social control, where students are taught to comply and to take up their place in an economy-driven world. In spite of significant effort over time to change this, policies and practices that continue to be most popular are those that industrialize schooling and undermine the well-being of individuals and their communities (e.g., zero tolerance; economic defunding of public education and inequitable distribution of resources; standardized grade levels, curriculum, and testing; and rewards-based learning).[3]

Rje is an invitation to create educational cultures that emphasize social engagement rather than social control.[4] The starting point in "how we are when we are together" is relationships rather than rules, people rather than policies, honoring capacity rather than evaluating ability, creating meaning rather than imposing knowledge, asking rather than telling, and well-being rather than merit-based success. This does not imply that rules, policies, evaluation, telling, and success are irrelevant; it simply means that these serve the needs of people living within community, not the other way around. Rje holds the possibility for changing learning factories into gardens where seeds are planted and growth is nurtured.

Summary

At its heart, rje invites educators to *engage with* students, students' parents/caregivers, colleagues, curriculum, educational institutions, community organizations, and the environment in a way that *honors* individuals in the context of their communities. In this way, as individuals and communities, everyone can thrive and grow to their full potential. As with any living entity, engagement requires shared caregiving and empowerment that *nurtures, feeds, guides,* and *supports*. It challenges traditional hierarchical power dynamics that expect educators to *manage, control, shape,* or *mold* students, as if they were inanimate objects. Rje creates spaces of shared learning and teaching.

Chapter 2:
An Important History of Restorative Justice in Education

Chapter 2 of the 2016 edition was titled "A Brief History of RJE." The last six years have shown us that the foundational principles of restorative justice embedded in history are leading rje advocates to places of deeper listening and to the realization that engaging with its history is critical for moving forward in healthy, just, and constructive ways. Thus, we retitled this chapter "An Important History of Restorative Justice in Education."

We maintain that this particular telling remains an incomplete history, bound by our own perspectives and experiences. It simply provides a starting point or an attempt, while knowing that there is much that has been unwritten.

* * *

Indigenous and Afro-Indigenous Roots of Restorative Justice Education

In 2021, Chief Mi'sel Joe of Miawpukek First Nation coined the term "two-eared listening" in his efforts to illustrate for non-Indigenous peoples of Newfoundland and Labrador what was at the core of restorative justice. "To understand justice," he said, "you need to hear the stories of injustice."[1] As he continued, he explained that when you hear the stories of injustice, you hear people sharing how their day-to-day lives have been disrupted, harmed, and destroyed, how the essence of who they are individually and communally has been assaulted. In both the sharing and then the listening with two ears, every part of us between those ears—bodies, hearts, and souls—is engaged. In this, we hear that *justice* is embodied in how we live together as community, how we support, encourage, and nurture each other. It is holistic, impacting all aspects of our society. This deep, interconnected, communal understanding of *justice* is difficult to understand in Western, Eurocentric societies that have reduced justice to the measurement of and response to the behavior of an individual or group as being right or fair. The important history of restorative justice begins with the reality that Indigenous and Afro-Indigenous communities over centuries of oppression have sustained this holistic understanding of justice that is rooted in community, relationships, and story.[2] Furthermore, this knowledge and way of being is still alive and well-practiced in many communities, despite the impacts of colonization. It is available for all of us to access and infuse into our lives, as the very people

17

who have suffered much harm are graciously inviting all of us who are immersed in a Western lifestyle of individualism to rethink our systemic and personal ways of being through restorative justice.[3]

These communal ways of being and their near erasure through colonization are well-documented, providing significant opportunities to listen with two ears. Circle dialogue, a practice foundational in most expressions of rje, needs to be more fully acknowledged and honored as deeply rooted within non-Western communities where they have long served as spaces for connection as well as solving the problems of the community *within the community.* Many Indigenous nations such as the Navajo people have historically viewed harm and conflict as a symptom of disconnection and have viewed justice through a lens of healing and reconnection—a restoration of relationships. Many, like the Maori nations in New Zealand, have incorporated variations of community-based sentencing and family group conferencing into their community practices for generations.

Though contemporary restorative justice and rje engage these practices in various ways, alongside Chief Mi'sel Joe, many are calling for a deeper understanding of restorative justice. Fania Davis, Edward Valandra, and Maisha Winn,[4] for example, amplify the reality that our current rje practices are often problematic as research shows that in many contexts, marginalized children and youth continue to be disproportionately[5] represented in suspensions, expulsions, office referrals, and special education programs, as well as restricted from having access to enrichment programming.[6] The same is true for

18

marginalized adults engaged in education systems who face discriminatory hiring and human resource concerns. To move forward, Valandra challenges us to address the first harms of land theft and slavery. If we are not working on that, then how can we model for children and youth how to engage in right relations? Rje advocates must expose that within the dominant, Western systems we function within, schooling has been and continues to be responsible for perpetuating privilege and undermining the creation of just and equitable environments. As the Truth and Reconciliation Commission of Canada presented its ninety-four recommendations in 2015,[7] and then again in the recent years when the mass and unmarked graves of hundreds of children and youth who died at state and church-run residential schools (1831–1996)[8] were identified and exposed, Honourable Justice Murray Sinclair said, "Education got us into this mess, education needs to get us out" (2015).[9] The history of rje also includes this call to recognize and address the deep oppression and harm brought on by colonization.

Faith-Based Foundations of Restorative Justice

Some religious traditions also align with the foundations of restorative justice, and there are many people of faith who believe restorative justice reflects the core beliefs and values of their faith tradition. In fact, many educational institutions' policies, procedures, and practices have deep roots drawing on faith-based "values" and assumptions. For example, Christian, Jewish, Hindu, Islamic, Buddhist, and Sikh belief systems all have sacred texts and practices that, depending on their interpretation, align well with the communal, relational core of restorative justice that honors all people as worthy. By contrast, other interpretations of those same sacred texts have led to a great deal of violence and harm. For example, it was members of the Christian tradition who interpreted their texts to justify acts of colonization—the process of settling among and establishing control over the Indigenous people of an area—and genocide.

For many rj and rje advocates who find meaning and purpose in faith and who have come to know rje initially through a faith context, this paradox between communal values (such as the worth and value of all) and the historic and ongoing oppression and rejection of those outside the faith tradition is difficult to reconcile. In some places, these intentional and unintentional misinterpretations and assumptions of sacred texts and teaching are being exposed so that the depth of the stories of injustice through faith/ religious practice can be heard.[10]

When rj is embraced as a way of healing, its values, beliefs, and practices might bring about opportunities for people of faith to struggle with this paradox, listening deeply to the pain of those who have been harmed by faith-based practices and calling our faith communities to participate in truth-telling, accountability, and restorative processes for the purpose of making things as right as possible.[11]

* * *

Whether visible or invisible, these important past and contemporary contexts are the soil within which the seed and roots of the current integration of restorative justice into education are growing. Maisha Winn helps to analyze the content of this soil by naming five pedagogical stances of rje: History Matters, Race Matters, Justice Matters, Language Matters, and Futures Matter.[12] There can be no restorative justice if the soil for the seeds is ignored, depleted, or taken for granted.

> To explore the quality of the "soil," read Chapter 2 in *Justice on Both Sides* by Maisha Winn.

Next, we look at what has occurred for rje to become part of schooling today. In knowing this whole story, rje advocates can better contribute to its critical development which has significant potential for nurturing more just, equitable, diverse, and inclusive cultures.

The Restorative Justice Foundations of RJE

Restorative justice, as a field in Western contexts, began in the criminal legal system. The Elmira (Ontario) Case of 1974 is generally accepted as the first Western application of restorative justice principles. This case began what became known as victim-offender reconciliation programs (VORP), which sought to find alternatives for addressing harm and responding to crime in ways that focused on relationships and healing rather than simply laws and punishment. In the Elmira case, a Canadian probation officer and a volunteer with the Mennonite Central Committee tried a more community-focused approach to a case involving two young men charged with vandalism. The two men were given the opportunity to meet with their victims and provide restitution. The outcome was a success. Modeled after the Elmira case, other victim-offender reconciliation programs were developed in both adult and youth criminal legal systems. VORP was introduced in the United States in Elkhart, Indiana, in the mid-1970s under the leadership of Howard Zehr, who has been a leader in the field of restorative justice for more than forty years. In 1990, Zehr authored *Changing Lenses: A New Focus for Crime and Justice,* now considered a seminal text of restorative justice, in which he provided a theoretical grounding for the growing work. Restorative justice continued to gain traction, becoming officially recognized by the American Bar Association in 1994 and by the United Nations in 1999.[13]

Expanding to the Educational Arena

The application of restorative justice principles and practices in schools has been recorded based on experiences primarily in Australia, New Zealand, Canada, the United States, and the United Kingdom. While rj was growing in the criminal legal arena, teachers, principals, and counselors began applying practices that had been found effective in the judicial system and adapting them to fit more closely within school contexts. For example, in 2000, a restorative justice partnership in British Columbia, Canada, emerged between the Community Justice

Initiatives Association and the Langley School District, bringing the practices of rj into schools. Similar community-school partnerships emerged across the globe, including in Pennsylvania and Colorado (USA), Queensland (Australia), Oxfordshire (England), and Wellington (New Zealand).

During this period of growth, Wendy Drewery (New Zealand) and Marg Thorsborne (Australia), as well as many others, built on Indigenous (Maori) practices and led the way in implementing family group conferences in school settings. Singapore and other parts of Asia also initiated peer mediation programs to address conflict and bullying, and the Safer School Partnerships arose in the United Kingdom, building on the restorative initiatives already being developed in schools by Belinda Hopkins and others since the mid-1990s.

The state of Minnesota (USA), under the leadership of Nancy Riestenberg, was a front-runner of restorative justice in school settings. Between 1998 and 2001, the Minnesota Department of Children, Families, and Learning began to work with schools to reduce suspensions and expulsions through the implementation of what were called restorative measures. Spurred on by the successes the schools were experiencing, the restorative justice work in Minnesota continued to grow into a statewide effort under the auspices of the Minnesota Department of Education (MN DoE). Riestenberg was hired by the MN DoE as a school climate specialist, responsible for supporting the implementation of restorative justice in Minnesota schools. Minnesota continues to embed restorative justice into school policies and practices and has provided a model for other schools, districts, and states seeking to implement rje. During the mid-2000s, several districts in Ontario, Canada (e.g., Waterloo, York) began hiring people to oversee the implementation of restorative justice practices in schools. Lynn Zammit, Angie Dornai, Brenda Morrison, and Jennifer Llewellyn were some of the early leaders in the rje movement in Canada.

A local Pennsylvania nonprofit, applying restorative justice principles in its work with students who had been expelled from school, established SaferSanerSchools in 1999. Out of that work, the International Institute for Restorative Practices (IIRP) emerged. The IIRP developed the first graduate-level program, accredited in 2007, that exclusively focused on teaching restorative practices. Besides developing its graduate school, the IIRP has established branches in Australia, Canada, Europe, and South America.

One of the things that complicates any attempt to devise a history of rje is the number of other programs, such as peace education, conflict resolution education, peer mediation, and restitution, that were also being developed to resolve school-based conflicts, to address the relational and learning needs of students, and to promote peacebuilding in schools. Throughout the 1980s and 1990s, before the term *restorative justice* had found its way into schools, these programs had been functioning effectively. As the language of restorative justice trickled into schools, the mingling of restorative justice with already existing programs was inevitable and, in many contexts, paved the way for a holistic understanding of restorative justice education to grow.

Columbine, Taber, and the Era of ZeroTolerance

As restorative justice was finding its way into schools, so too, were zero tolerance policies. In 1994, the Gun-Free Schools Act (GFSA) was passed in the United States, and in 2000 the Safe Schools Act (SSA) was passed in Ontario, Canada. The concept of zero tolerance had been connected to the criminal legal system for years, representing a "get tough on crime" mentality. With the GFSA and the SSA, the language of zero tolerance found its way into schools, creating more draconian approaches to school discipline. Initially, policies in both countries called for mandatory suspensions for any weapons possession on school campuses; eventually, it was expanded to include drug possessions and a host of other offenses.

In 1999, two events led to a full-scale ramping up of those draconian measures: on April 20, in Columbine, Colorado, USA, two students opened fire at Columbine High School, killing thirteen and injuring twenty-one others. Eight days later, a fourteen-year-old student walked into a high school in Taber, Alberta, Canada, and shot another youth in what appeared to be an attempt to replicate the Columbine attack. In the years following those two school shootings, the application of zero tolerance policies escalated to include a host of school behaviors, increasing the use of suspensions and expulsions, and laying the foundation for what has often been called the school-to-prison pipeline.[14] After a few years of the "zero-tolerance frenzy,"[15] the general population began to seriously question the policies' effectiveness, and many schools began to look for other ways to address issues arising in schools.

From Zero Tolerance to Restorative Justice

The increasing critique of zero tolerance made way for new restorative justice initiatives. For example, in 2007, the Minister of Education for Ontario in Canada announced that zero tolerance had been a failure and initiated legislation that would replace zero tolerance policies with student supports, such as mediation and restorative justice.[16] Likewise, in the United States, the American Psychological Association published a report arguing that zero tolerance policies were not only ineffective but also stood in direct opposition to what was known about child development and best practices in education.[17]

In 2014, the US Department of Justice and the US Department of Education issued a joint statement that exclusionary discipline was being overused and applied in discriminatory ways. They recommended the use of restorative justice as one of many alternatives to suspensions and expulsions.[18] In the wake of these shifts, there has been a growing awareness and acceptance of rj in educational contexts. Rather than a teacher here and a school counselor there, entire school districts have worked to adopt rj practices.

Of note has been the Oakland-based RJOY in the United States, led by Rita Alfred, Fania Davis, and John Kidde. Drawing on the resources of RJOY, Cole Middle School in West Oakland began initiating rj training for teachers and other school personnel in 2005 at the prompting of the school's disciplinary case manager. By 2007, rj had become the primary system for addressing discipline issues at Cole, and students were being trained as circle facilitators. As of 2016, the Oakland district maintained a central rj office and had an rj coordinator in almost every middle and high school. The trend of replacing discipline systems away from zero tolerance continues. See Recent Shifts in RJE (page 30) for more information.

Early (and Ongoing) Conversations in RJE

Restorative justice in educational contexts, though still often referenced in connection to the broader rj field, solidified as a field of its own with its own practices and principles between 2010 and 2015 after a decade of documenting the learning that arose from early implementation efforts. Three early shifts could be identified.

1. The development of education-specific rj theory

Early restorative justice work in schools was a grassroots movement led by teachers, counselors, and principals. As it grew, it became increasingly more systematized and integrated into schools as institutions. Although there was some theory undergirding the early practices, that theory primarily emerged from the disciplines of criminology and sociology—not necessarily from education. The need for rje to develop as a field of its own challenged advocates to seek out deeper foundations in educational theory integrated with pedagogical considerations. One of the implications of this growth was an increasing need for resources and research. Some

27

educators started to write about education-specific rj theory in the first decade of the twenty-first century. Hopkins (2004) wrote about whole-school approaches to rj implementation, asserting that creating *Just Schools* required more than just responses to disciplinary infractions. Stutzman Amstutz and Mullet (2005) wrote *The Little Book of Restorative Discipline for Schools*, laying out foundational principles for applying restorative justice to school-based discipline incidents. Several books focusing on restorative justice in school contexts were published in 2007. The Claassens published *Discipline That Restores*, providing a model for school discipline and strategies for creating more respectful and cooperative learning environments. Morrison wrote the first comprehensive academic account of the development of restorative justice as a response to bullying and school violence in *Restoring Safe School Communities*. In addition to some of the written resources, the availability of videos and other tools for implementation increased. (A list of resources is included at the end of this book.)

2. An expanded understanding of rje

Initially, the application of restorative justice to school-based situations was primarily an attempt to find alternatives to suspensions and expulsions. Most restorative justice programs focused on student behaviors and finding ways for students to address the harm they caused. As the process revealed how behaviors occurred in a context, rje grew to include ways to nurture healthy school climates in holistic and proactive ways. Morrison and Vaandering[19] began to frame students' behavior through a lens of social engagement as opposed to social control, echoing educational research that encouraged shifts in school climate instead of simply trying to change individual student behaviors.

Thus, although some continued to view restorative justice as a menu of interventions to address harm, conflict, and student behaviors, many began to recognize the need for rje to be a theoretical framework through which to view not only the repairing of harm, but also the restoration of healthy community relationships that thrive in just and equitable learning environments. In practice, this was often supported through the connection of social-emotional learning (SEL) to rje, emphasizing the need for explicit engagement with recognizing, naming, and responding to emotions.

3. The emergence of rje within teacher preparation programs

The growth of rje gradually evolved from only short professional development or community-based trainings to its inclusion in teacher preparation programs. Early teacher education programs offering courses and certificates on restorative justice included the University of Waikato in New Zealand (2000).[20] In 2014, Eastern Mennonite University in Harrisonburg, Virginia, USA, initiated the first graduate-level rje program specifically located in a teacher education department, offering both an MA in education with a concentration in rje and a graduate certificate in rje.[21] In 2015, Simon Fraser University in Vancouver, British Columbia, Canada, followed suit, approving the development of an rje program in an education department.[22] In more recent years, this growth in teacher education programs continues globally. The importance for educators to be equipped with the knowledge, skills, and dispositions required to lead restorative justice implementation is now well-documented, resulting in similar programs becoming more common.

Recent Shifts in RJE

Since 2016, rje has grown significantly. Theory, expanded perspectives, and education programs continue to develop globally and, along with these, the potential for rje's role in transforming education is becoming more obvious. The following more recent shifts are important to note:

A Growing Body of Research Revealing Key Components of Authentic Practice

Since 2016, research documenting the impact of rje is flourishing. The insights gained reveal both promising and concerning outcomes that are now guiding further development of rje's principles and practices. A recent informative review (Gregory & Evans, 2020)[23] indicates that as with all initiatives in their early stages, there are clear examples of strong starts as well as those that can only be characterized as serious stumbles. Most humbling has been the revelation that rje has not yet effectively addressed disproportionate representation of minority populations. Students of color, students with disabilities, and LGBTQ+ students continue to experience higher-than-average rates of suspensions and expulsions relative to their peers. Reviews such as this one must inform the current growth of rje.

Anti-Racist, Culturally Informed Principles and Practices

Since 2016, there has been an honest critique about how rje in mainstream institutions exhibits appropriation and co-opting of Indigenous and Afro-Indigenous ways of being. This increase in literature cannot be ignored and needs to be highlighted, acknowledged, and addressed in authentically equitable ways by rje advocates moving forward. As the field of rje is learning to listen more intentionally to advocates who represent communities of Indigenous, Black, and People of Color, it has become very clear that when implemented in schools, rje must be intentional about creating equitable spaces where race and culture are not appropriated, tokenized, or patronized. Education as a colonized and colonizing experience can be addressed through rje that truly honors all people as worthy and interconnected. However, without explicit awareness, rje can also remain a colonizing experience.[24]

An Increased Emphasis on Trauma and Resilience

Researchers and practitioners alike have recently highlighted the need for rje practices to be informed by greater awareness of how trauma, in all its forms, shows up in relationships. Joe Brummer's book, *Building a Trauma-Informed Restorative School*,[25] is foundational for recognizing how educators easily overlook the role of trauma in the lives of their

31

students, families, and colleagues. When this occurs, the practice of rje can actually cause further harm. When rje is understood as a framework for being and practiced holistically, trauma-informed practice is woven throughout and becomes the way we do things in education.

Summary

Rje is growing rapidly. In this chapter, we have situated this growth within a historical context; without understanding that history, we believe there is great risk in ongoing development that will continue to cause harm. As rje becomes more established, we need to listen with two ears to those who are most vulnerable to the impact of rje. To do this well, we must be guided by the very essence of what Indigenous and Afro-Indigenous peoples call us to do, to become aware of and explicitly engage with the core beliefs and values that guide this work.

The original content of the LB of RJE explicitly discussed this need. What has been confirmed since its publication is just how important this is. This new edition affirms the comprehensive view of rje as a framework, not simply as a set of practices. Chapter 3 explores these core beliefs and values and provides opportunities to engage with them through relevant questions and activities.

Chapter 3: Beliefs and Values in RJE

Think about a decision, big or small, that you made recently and the actions that followed. Now consider which factors influenced your decision:
- Were you influenced by other people?
- Were you influenced by perceptions of the situation?
- Were you influenced by possible consequences?
- Were you influenced by previous experiences?

Decision-making is a part of life. When life is routine, it is as natural as breathing, eating, and sleeping; we rarely consider what influences how we make choices unless the consequences of that decision surprise us. This is like attending to the flower of a plant and forgetting that growth begins with a seed and depends on roots. Similarly, the seeds and roots of decision-making and actions by a person, an organization, an institution, or a society are reflective of beliefs and values.

In the past years, during which we all experienced the impact of the pandemic, racial tensions, war, economic restrictions, climate change, and so much more, identifying and discussing beliefs and values became more explicit. We more readily recognized when our beliefs and values aligned or clashed with those of our friends and neighbors because of our responses to protests, health regulations, or social media.

From these recent experiences, seeing how rje has grown from a particular set of beliefs and values is more obvious. To successfully implement, nurture, and sustain rje, it is necessary to assess if and how personal and organizational beliefs and values line up with those of rje. Beliefs and values are often assumed, varied, interconnected, and influenced by our sociocultural contexts. Identifying and assessing these beliefs and values can be difficult, yet positive social change requires that this be done.

In this chapter, we adopt another metaphor, the use of eyeglasses, as a way to better recognize our beliefs and values. We further define what we mean by rje beliefs and values, invite readers to identify personal core beliefs and values, and illustrate how rje lives out its beliefs and values.

The Glasses That Shape Our View of the World

Howard Zehr, in describing the foundations of restorative justice, explains that engaging with rj requires that we examine and change the lenses through which we are seeing the world.[1] Just as properly prescribed eyeglasses help us see things more clearly, so, too, does explicitly articulating our perspectives help us make sense of the world. Our perspectives come from our beliefs and values. Like the frames and lenses of a pair of glasses, beliefs hold values, and values support beliefs. Together they impact our decisions and actions.

Beliefs, the frames of our glasses, are specific ideas we accept as true that cannot be fully proven. Although they are often based on experiential evidence or intuition, beliefs also involve feelings of trust and conviction. Beliefs impact our view of the world. Beliefs can include the acceptance of things that happened in the distant past (e.g., dinosaurs) or will happen in the future (e.g., end result of a climate crisis), trust in a theory or things unseen (e.g., the big bang theory), faith in supreme beings (e.g., religions), or the conviction of our purpose as people (e.g., individualism). We are introduced to these beliefs from the time we are born, through personal experiences within our families and other sociocultural contexts.

Some of what we believe is rarely questioned. At other times, experiences cause us to confront our beliefs and we decide to accept, adjust, or reject them for new beliefs. Whether they are conscious or unconscious, beliefs shape how we think and act. They become the framework, mindset, or *perspective* that guides how we live. For example, do we believe that children and youth are miniature adults with a fully developed rational capacity to understand their choices and actions, *or* do we view them as people whose capacity to understand is still developing? In this instance, what we believe about children and youth will influence how we interact with them.

Values, the lenses of the glasses that we look through, represent what we think is important about life. They emerge from our beliefs and can also influence our beliefs. Values come into being through our interactions with others, our environment, and our desire for well-being. As individuals, we know what we need to survive and thrive and will make choices that we believe will nurture our well-being. Returning to the example of how we view children and youth, if we believe them to be miniature adults, we may presume that their actions are intentional and that reprimands and punishment will result in change. Thinking about them as developing people, we presume that their actions indicate they are struggling to handle something difficult and they need support. The first perspective includes values such as obedience, perfection, compliance, and assimilation. The second includes values such as honesty, trust, encouragement, support, relationship, and collaboration.

How do we put on glasses that will allow us to understand rje? First, we become aware of the fact that we are each wearing a particular pair of glasses that shapes how we see the world. Then, we see the options available for a different pair. Finally, we choose to take off the old and put on the new.

What Glasses Am I Wearing?

What we believe and value might not always be clear. In fact, what we say we believe and value might actually be different from reality. Sometimes beliefs and values are unconscious; other times they are suppressed because they seem to conflict with those of the community. Ultimately, our actions, not our words, most accurately reflect what is at our core. We live up to our beliefs, not to what we say we believe.[2] Deep reflection is needed to bring core beliefs and values to the surface.

One way to do so is to examine our actions. By identifying the values reflected in our actions, we can connect values to core beliefs. Try one or more of these:

- Think of someone in your life you care deeply about. Make a list of what you would miss about that person if you were separated.
- Think of a group of people you engage with through your work or personal life. Make a list of the things you need *from them* to be your best self.
- Find an object that represents *hope* for you. List the things that influenced your choice.

Consider what you have listed. These begin to identify your values. Now choose one value and consider what it indicates about what you believe about people. For example, if you *value affirmation* from others to be your best self, it may point to your *belief* that people are *interconnected* and that we need one another to be fully human.

This is but a beginning experience with a very complex process. Our glasses are also shaped by the groups we are a part of that represent our various identities, such as race, ethnicity, religion, sexuality, gender, ability, class, etc. For example:

- We are both white, middle-class, able-bodied professors with European origins who hold a great deal of privilege. That privilege shapes the glasses we wear, whether or not we like it. When we become aware of our glasses, we can begin to see how our beliefs and values might undermine the well-being of others.
- Many Western societies today are strongly influenced by ideals that elevate individual freedom and free-market economies in pursuit of profit. Educational organizations within these societies typically operate using a corporate model, in which students become commodities, objectified as having value only when they produce meet academic standards as defined by test scores.[3]

The complexity involved in identifying beliefs and values can be overwhelming. Simply beginning, however, is important. It will reveal what, if any, distorted views we unwittingly hold. If there is a disconnect between beliefs, values, and actions, don't be discouraged. It's normal and actually better positions us to look for other options. Deep reflection provides the foundation for authentic, sustainable change.

New Glasses

The principles and practices of restorative justice in education are supported by two key beliefs:

- Human beings are *worthy.*
- Human beings are *interconnected* with each other and the world.[4]

Regardless of someone's visible characteristics or actions, that person is of worth simply because he or she is a living, breathing human being. People thrive when they are in good relationships with others and their environments. People are interconnected.

Surrounding these beliefs are three core values: respect, dignity, and mutual concern.[5] Respect and dignity speak directly to honoring the worth of people. Mutual concern speaks to our interconnectedness. In considering whether our actions align with these values, we might ask the following questions:

- In my interactions with others and the world, do I give respect by *accepting* them for who they are, or do I want to change them to be more like me or like someone who will meet my needs?
- Do I *treat others with dignity,* engaging fully to highlight the best in them?
- Do I notice what others need to survive and thrive?
- Do I ensure that I am not interfering with another person's well-being?
- Do I engage with people to ensure that their well-being is nurtured and that they can flourish?
- Can I see how my answers to these questions reflect my relationship with myself?

These values encapsulate what it is to be human from an rje perspective and therefore point to the reality that in order to flourish, we need to *belong.* Thus, if externally you are treated as worthy (you are

Respect (re: again; *spect:* to look): "To look again" from the point of view of the other; to put one's self in the other's shoes and then respond.

allowed to be connected to others), internally you experience *belonging* (you know what it is to feel secure). From an rje perspective, we accept that we do not always enact our beliefs and values flawlessly. However, being aware of this allows us to address harms without fear, confident that our worth and interconnectedness will be upheld even in tension.

How Do We Put on Our RJE Glasses?

At times, we can be myopic, thinking that we personally have a clearer perspective than others have. For example, we might convince ourselves that we do *respect* self, others, and the world we live in. Yet, how we define and experience respect may be quite different from how others do so. The variations in who we are as people make living relationally complex. So then, how can we put on the glasses of rje? One approach we have found helpful invites us to reflect critically on our own interactions with others by answering three questions:

Dignity: Worth that cannot be substituted. People have dignity because the essence of who they are cannot be replaced.

1. Am I honoring?
2. Am I measuring?
3. What message am I sending?[6]

Mutual concern: Much more than a common concern, mutual concern is reciprocal, interconnected caring.

Am I Honoring?

Honoring people is a way of accepting others for who they are. It requires that I consider whether I am aware of the needs, perspectives, and cultures of others as fully as I am aware of my own. It also requires careful asking and listening, trusting others and dispensing with a desire to "fix" or "help" them. Belonging and support are nurtured when I am willing to be present with another without judging that person.

Am I Measuring?

Measuring people is a way of judging others (or myself) to see if they fit my expectation of who I think they *should* be. Measuring places me in a position of power where my own worth is affirmed by someone else's lack of ability or worth. The perceived inadequacies of the other validate my own worth.

We are encouraged constantly within Western society to measure one another and to form groups that welcome some and marginalize others. For example, commerce creates divisions between those who "have" and those who "have not." Through advertising, we are made to feel inferior or superior based on ownership of the latest gadgets and fashions. Schools, in a similar way, are designed to label and group students based on ability and behavior. Comparisons and assessment may be necessary and helpful, but when we do measure, it is important to determine the purpose of measuring. For example, we might ask, "Is my measurement of Sasha's ability to read nurturing her well-being or primarily a way of highlighting my capacity to teach well?"

It can be presumptuous to think we can identify what constitutes someone's well-being. How can I really be sure that my actions are contributing to worthiness and interconnectedness of others? Thus, the next question gives others the opportunity to provide feedback about our interaction.

What Message Am I Sending?

This question requires empathy and compassion. Either I empathetically put myself in the other's shoes in an attempt to understand our interaction, or I compassionately ask the other directly whether they considered our engagement honoring. All of our words and actions send messages to the people we are with that assure them of how or if they belong. We won't fully know the messages we are sending unless we ask.

Living with RJE Glasses

Putting on rje glasses by examining our interactions with others may feel odd at first. As we grow, the three questions remind us of our changing perspectives, and we may find it tiring to continuously be this reflective. Though the view may be clearer, we may find it distinctively different from our regular view. At times, the discrepancy between our new view and what we used to experience is magnified.

42

We may need to take off our new glasses at times because of the discomfort. However, as we experience more authentic relationships, we will find ourselves reaching for them. In time we will no longer be as conscious of our "new" view. Wearing rje glasses is a relief in that honoring the worth and interconnectedness of all people with respect, dignity, and mutual concern usually resonates with who we are personally. With an rje perspective, we come to acknowledge each other's vulnerabilities and contributions. Fear of conflict and difference diminishes. Instead of becoming protective and defensive, we engage with one another to find ways to move forward so that everyone's well-being is nurtured. Ultimately, living with rje glasses allows us to look at life as an opportunity for social engagement rather than social control.[7]

Summary

This chapter highlights the need to identify and examine if/how personal beliefs and values resonate with those of rje. In addition, it also challenges us to examine how rje beliefs and values align with the core beliefs and values of educational institutions. Understanding how these resonate or differ from each other will shape how rje is developed and sustained.

This chapter invited you to engage actively with challenging concepts. What did you discover as you worked through the activities? Revisiting these will provide clarity when necessary. As authors, we do this regularly. It causes discomfort but it is the very thing that continues to call us "up" to the values that we hope to live into.

Returning to the analogy of the plant, this chapter explores the seed (beliefs) and the initial roots (values) of rje. Without them there would be no way to anchor or feed the principles and practices of rje that are expressed explicitly through creating just and equitable learning environments, nurturing healthy relationships, and repairing harm and transforming conflict.

SECTION 2
Examining the Components of Restorative Justice in Education

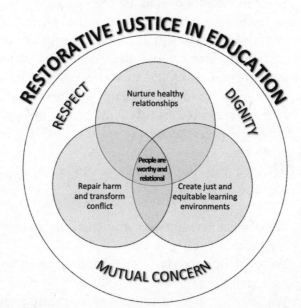

Chapter 3 articulates the central belief that all people are worthy and relational as a foundational tenet of restorative justice in education (rje), encircled by the key values of respect, dignity, and mutual concern. In Section 2 we move to look at the three core components of rje.

- Chapter 4 discusses the importance of creating just and equitable learning environments.
- Chapter 5 examines the explicit nurturing of healthy relationships.
- Chapter 6 explains the comprehensive nature of repairing harm and transforming conflict.

As illustrated in the preceding diagram, the three components of rje not only intersect but also revolve around the same hub of core beliefs and values. Concepts discussed in each of the following three chapters overlap with and inform the others. For example, a key to nurturing healthy relationships is the establishment of just and equitable learning environments *and* an ability to assess power dynamics in relationships to productively address conflict and harm. Intertwined in this way, one is not more important or a prerequisite for another. All of them are essential.

In Section 2, the chapters share a similar three-part structure. For each chapter,

1. We discuss terminology and the importance of the topic for school culture.
2. We explain how rje informs and engages with each component.
3. We provide concrete actions steps that support educators in implementing the component comprehensively.

These action steps are not exhaustive but are meant to serve as possible starting points for applying the foundational concepts. Rje is dependent on context. As you begin to engage with the concepts and activities in these chapters, more concrete action steps that match the unique needs and gifts of your school community will emerge. Additionally, each chapter contains various "callout boxes" that provide questions, activities, thoughts, or suggestions for consideration. These can be used individually or in groups and are intended to support efforts for making each concept a reality.

Chapter 4:
Creating Just and Equitable Learning Environments

Before you begin reading, take a moment to jot down some words or pictures that come to mind when you think about justice and equity. How do you imagine these ideas playing out in school settings? What is educational justice? What is an equitable learning environment? How is justice applied and experienced in your educational context?

Creating just and equitable learning environments is complex. It requires a clear understanding of justice and equity, as well as an awareness of injustice. However, understanding and awareness alone are insufficient. Intentional collaboration, education, self-reflection, and a commitment to the beliefs and values discussed in Chapter 3 are necessary, as are nurturing healthy relationships (Chapter 5) and cultivating the ability to address conflict and harm (Chapter 6).

49

Consider the following scenarios:

- Cade struggled to sound out the word *categorize* on the state-mandated mathematics exam. As an eighth grader, failing this exam would mean they would have to start their high school math sequence with pre-algebra, which would prevent them from taking the necessary math courses to earn a college prep diploma. They were good in math; they just couldn't read this word.

- Terry just accepted a position as a fifth-grade language arts teacher. While his public school cannot legally fire him based on his sexual orientation, recent legislation has created policy that prevents him from talking with his students about his husband or their two children. Furthermore, he fears that if students, parents, or other teachers find out that he is gay, he may face social alienation or increased scrutiny about his performance. As a result, he remains silent and avoids conversations related to his personal life.

- Kali walked into his third-grade classroom on a Monday early in December to find a brightly lit tree, a large picture of Santa Claus on the wall, and Christmas music playing softly in the background. He sighed, feeling slightly out of place, and worried that the other children would find out that his family doesn't celebrate Christmas.

Defining Justice and Equity

Everyday, many children and educators go to school and find themselves in situations where the deck is stacked against them. Some of them feel marginalized based on race, gender, or sexual orientation. Others experience school as disconnected from their lives due to language, religion, social class, or ability. To understand this reality more fully, it is important to grasp the essence of justice and equity.

Justice

Attempts to define the concept of justice are met with significant challenges; the word itself has been used in different ways and has been employed to mean anything from a person who acts as a judge (e.g., chief justice) to a system for enforcing a set of laws (e.g., the criminal justice system) to a way of distributing resources among people (e.g., social justice). As a result of the ways in which the word *justice* has been employed to mean so many things, some opt to use different language when talking about *restorative justice* (rj).

For example, some restrict the use of the term *restorative justice* to reactive responses to crime and wrongdoing, while others prefer the language of *restorative discipline* to indicate a specific approach to addressing behavioral concerns. Various other terms have been created to indicate more proactive practices designed to build community within and beyond educational settings, such as *restorative approaches* or *restorative practices*.

While we honor the work of those who use other terminology, we hold on to the term *justice* as a way to highlight the comprehensive nature of primary justice in rje, which is about the reciprocal pursuit of what everyone needs for their individual and collective well-being. It embraces respect, dignity, and mutual concern as a way to honor the worth of all (e.g., they experienced justice). This definition of justice encompasses much more than secondary justice, which addresses behavior and administering consequences to people who do wrong (e.g., justice was served). It includes examining asymmetrical relationships and finding ways to provide for the needs of everyone in those relationships. These ideas are well grounded in a variety of traditions.

Howard Zehr equates *justice* with the Hebrew word shalom. Here, justice is about "right" relationships in which "right" refers to things as they are supposed to be. Relatedly, the Hebrew word *sedeqah* is about "right" living or righteousness. When we seek to live in shalom, *sedeqah* is the act of doing justice. *Sedeqah* does not indicate a passive stance but rather an active, engaged doing of justice. Thus, within the Judeo-Christian tradition, *justice* is about the "positive presence of harmony and wholeness, of health and prosperity, of integration and balance . . . the state of soundness or flourishing in all dimensions of existence."[1]

Islam holds similar ideas about peace and justice. Amir Akrami, a theological scholar from Yale Divinity School, notes that the word *salaam* refers to a sense of peace, health, and wholeness. Incorporating this word into a common greeting, *assalamu alaikum* conveys a desire for peace and wholeness to the recipient of the greeting. The Arabic word *adala* is most closely aligned with the concept of justice and denotes the Quranic concept of "putting things in their right and appropriate place, where they are supposed to be."[2]

Likewise, justice and equity are foundational within Indigenous traditions. The medicine wheel in native spirituality, for example, symbolizes balance

52

and harmony. In addition, the word *namwayut* (from the Musqueam people), meaning "we are all one," points us to the importance of living in balance and harmony with one another. When we live *namwayut,* we acknowledge the interdependence of humanity and work to ensure that relationships are healthy and that reconciliation occurs in ways that are just. The Honorable Chief Justice Dr. Robert Yazzie of the Navajo Nation differentiates between horizontal justice and vertical justice. Within vertical justice, the offender and the victim are seen as separate and detached; the outcomes are defined by winning and losing. Within horizontal justice, equality is like a circle in which no one is more important than another. We are all one. The outcome of justice is related to wholeness and healing rather than right and wrong. Furthermore, helping another person is more important than determining fault. Responsibility lies with each of us to repair harm and restore justice.[3]

> Take a moment and think about the spiritual or moral traditions that ground your understanding of justice, equity, and wholeness. How do the concepts of rje align with those traditions?

Within these traditions, there is a close connection between the concepts of justice and peace. According to criminologist Elizabeth Elliott, "A peaceful, safe and just society begins with individuals who are at

53

peace with themselves living in peaceful interactions with others."[4] Without a sense of peace, where harmony among all is realized, there isn't really any justice. Conversely, without a sense of justice, peace is difficult to achieve. Ursula Franklin, a physicist and peace activist, defined peace as the absence of fear and suggested that by overcoming oppression, justice creates a world where there is no need to fear another.[5] Thus, for rje, any attempt at building peace requires that justice be an essential component.

In summary, Carolyn Boyes-Watson and Kay Pranis remind us that justice is not about laws or defined behaviors, but rather about relationships. They argue that human beings have a strong, innate sense of things that are just and equitable. When our relationships are experienced as unjust, we can build up "negative emotions, such as anger, resentment, distrust and humiliation that often motivate people to take action to correct the imbalance or injustice." Conversely, when relationships are viewed as just, we experience "a sense of harmony, peace, stability, and satisfaction."[6]

Equity

Equity means fairness or impartiality. Unlike equality, which suggests that everyone is treated the same or gets the same share, equity focuses on equal outcomes and requires that everyone gets what they need in order to experience well-being. We often assume that in order to be fair, everyone has to be treated the same. That would be fine if we all started from the same place—but we don't.

The crucial difference between equity and equality can be illustrated by looking at zero tolerance policies in school settings. In the early 1990s, zero tolerance policies were implemented, claiming to be fairer than preceding disciplinary policies because all students were to be treated exactly the same. For example, in a situation in which two students got into a fistfight, zero tolerance policies required that both be suspended from school for ten days, regardless of the circumstances. Supposedly, a predetermined consequence would prevent disparities, leveling the playing field for all students.

As research has shown, however, zero tolerance policies not only failed to make schools safer but actually exacerbated unequal treatment.[7] Despite the rhetoric about treating everyone equally, these policies grossly exacerbated disproportionate (i.e., inequitable) discipline rates for students of color, those coming from economically disadvantaged families, those placed in special education, and LGBTQ students.[8] In attempting to treat everyone the same, schools overlooked factors such as bullying, school failure, trauma, racism, etc., that impacted students' behaviors. By ignoring the needs arising from these injustices, many students weren't actually treated fairly at all. The policies intended to create equality actually led to an objectification of students, as though the incidents leading to disciplinary responses were disconnected from everything else in their life.

Equity, in contrast to equality, asks this question: What do people need in order to experience well-being?

Returning to the zero tolerance example, the two students who got into a fight might have done so for vastly different reasons, representing different needs.

Let's imagine that for one student, the fight was due to underlying academic frustration that then erupted in the cafeteria; for the other, the fight was in retaliation for being bullied earlier in the day. Although theoretically treated "equally" in that they were both suspended for ten days, they weren't treated equitably—neither got what he needed. Furthermore, the needs of others who were impacted by the fight—students and staff—were completely ignored.

There is a temptation to assume that because something seems just and fair to us, it should be obviously so for others. The problem with that reasoning is that people's sense of what is just and fair varies. When people say, "That's not fair," it is important to have a respectful dialogue to understand their notion of justice. What is it about their experience that feels unjust for them? We don't have to share their perspective, but if we are going to be effective at addressing their frustration, we must at least try to understand it.

In an rje school, a focus on justice and equity creates space for understanding and for addressing

> Let's wrestle with the word *fair* for a minute. When a student complains, "That's not fair," what he likely means is that someone else got something he didn't. He's talking about equality. How might we instead create an environment of equity where well-being, not sameness, is our goal?

underlying needs that often manifest in challenging behavior. In the preceding example, a focus on justice and equity would potentially have prevented the fight from happening in the first place. By working to ensure that one student received appropriate academic support while the other had a safe place to address the bullying, needs would have been met prior to behaviors escalating.

In the rest of this chapter, we provide additional examples demonstrating how rje practices can work to promote just and equitable learning environments.

How RJE Addresses Issues of Justice and Equity

In this section, we discuss ways that schools implementing rje might address issues of injustice and inequity. There is a long history of educators seeking more just and equitable ways of doing school. For example, the National Council of Teachers of English (NCTE) has included an emphasis on social justice and equity in its standards for the preparation of teachers.[9] Resources such as *Reading, Writing, and Rising Up: Teaching about Social Justice and the Power of the Written Word* by Linda Christensen

> Review the core values of rje: respect, dignity, and mutual concern. As you read this section, note places where these values are enacted (e.g., relationships, policies, school routines).

focus on teaching social justice to students using content-area curriculum. Publications such as *Rethinking Schools* and *Learning for Justice* provide extensive resources for educators who desire to include more socially just pedagogy in their practices. Resources such as these can support the work of rje to nurture more just and equitable school environments.

Promoting Just and Equitable Relationships

Because rje is a relational framework, school-based relationships should be characterized by justice and equity. Restorative justice processes are designed to facilitate relationships in which everyone is treated with worth and dignity, regardless of their race, ethnicity, religion, nationality, ability, economic class, language, body type, gender, or sexual orientation. For example, circle processes allow for everyone in the circle to have an opportunity to speak from their own experience. In the circle, no one is more important than another and everyone's perspectives are respected. Likewise, when harm occurs, restorative conferencing is primarily a space for those harmed to have their needs met; this further ensures upholding the worth and dignity of all. Those causing harm are held accountable and have the opportunity to contribute to the healing process where possible.

Restorative justice practices create spaces to be heard, but part of building a restorative ethos in a school is creating those spaces in less structured ways. According to Kay Pranis, "Justice is not about getting even, but rather about getting well." One way we can help our students experience healing is by listening to them. This is particularly true for students who have often been marginalized or who have experienced school as a harmful place. For all students, but for these students in particular, taking time to meet with them during or after school to hear about what is important in their lives will create a relationship that supports them. This simple act of reaching out has the potential to preempt the meltdown they may have had later in your biology class.

Addressing Underlying Needs

Just and equitable outcomes means working to ensure that people get what they need. According to criminologists Dennis Sullivan and Larry Tifft, "We develop our potentialities as human beings and enhance our collective well-being when our needs are respected, expressed, listened to, defined with care, and ultimately met."[10] One of the core principles of rje is a commitment to addressing the needs of all of those in the community, including students, educators, and families. Even when those needs cannot be met fully, there is still value in the acknowledgment of those needs.

The importance of acknowledging underlying needs is not new within educational theory, including the work of Nel Noddings, Carl Rogers, and Abraham Maslow. It is important to note, however, that the ideas represented predate modern educational theory. Abraham Maslow's ideas can be traced to his experiences and research while living with the Blackfoot Nation and learning about their way of being in community. He noted their commitment to ensuring that everyone in their tribe had what they needed. His writings about the Hierarchy of Needs are drawn directly from the Indigenous wisdom of the Blackfoot people who acknowledged that self-actualization was the base of the triangle, but that the aim of humankind was care for community and the perpetuation of cultural values. Years of educational research affirm this principle that we all thrive more when the needs of all members of the community are met. For example, the work of Deci and Ryan articulates several "universal" core needs that drive motivation:

1. **Autonomy:** a sense of control over our own destiny
2. **Belonging:** the assurance that we are accepted, valued, and respected
3. **A sense of competence:** the assurance that we are capable[11]

Similarly, Howard Zehr articulated three core needs that serve as pillars of rj and that are fundamental for well-being:

1. **Autonomy:** a sense of personal control and empowerment
2. **Order:** a sense of trust about the world we live in and how it works
3. **Relatedness:** a sense of connection and where we fit in our relationships

Zehr says that when those core needs are not met, "we may construct a world in which we establish a sense of *autonomy* by domination over others, an *order* based on violence and force, and a sense of *relatedness* rooted in distrust of others and kinship with fellow 'outsiders.'"[12] For example, a student who feels that she doesn't have any friends may resort to illicit behavior in order to gain a sense of belonging. Attempts to control the student's behavior may end up exacerbating the problem by taking from her the very control that she is working so diligently to obtain. Conversely, creating a school culture of belonging and dignity for all might meet her need for relationships in ways that promote healing, justice, and belonging.

Rje is about addressing underlying needs. For example, consider students' need for autonomy. In schools committed to rje, there is an emphasis on shared decision making and a commitment to *power with* rather than *power over.* (See Chapter 5 for more details). Rje recognizes that people are capable of making good decisions. Sometimes they need guidance, but that should never prevent them from being involved in making decisions about their future, about their behavior, and about their academics.

Rje acknowledges the learning needs of students and the importance of instruction that promotes the active engagement of all learners. Drawing on Paulo Freire's work, restorative educators resist the "banking model" of education, in which students are passive recipients of the teacher's knowledge; instead, the prior knowledge and experiences of all learners are considered valuable for learning.[13] Students are taught within their zone of proximal development,[14] and instruction is differentiated according to content, process, product, affect, and environment.[15] Acknowledging that all students bring worth to our classrooms, an rje framework seeks to address the

61

underlying social, emotional, and academic needs of each student.

Explicitly Addressing Injustices

As many schools become increasingly diverse, there has been an increased awareness of the need to implement culturally responsive pedagogy.[16] Unfortunately, initiatives that promote cultural competence, intercultural teaching, and multicultural education have too often been limited to discussions about foods, dress, and dance. Furthermore, they have been restricted to certain months of the school year or specific aspects of the curriculum. As Paul Gorski and Katy Swalwell warn, too often "diversity initiatives avoid or whitewash serious equity issues."[17]

We can't just talk about welcoming or valuing diversity without acknowledging that many students who fall outside of the dominant majority experience unaddressed discrimination and marginalization daily. For example, as noted earlier, discipline statistics over the past forty years reveal a gross disparity between white students and students of color. Even the most student-centered discipline policies too often focus on helping students become more like the dominant majority and fail to address implicit bias that is often woven into curriculum and school practices. Disparities also show up in enrollment in advanced placement and honors classes; white students are more likely to have access to and enroll in those classes than students of color.[18]

When schools and classrooms perpetuate racial or ethnic discrimination, whether intentional or not, we should expect students to feel disconnected, disengaged, and defiant. Rje prioritizes justice and equity where

- the vulnerable are cared for,
- the marginalized are included,
- the dignity and humanity of each person in the educational setting matters, and
- everyone's needs are heard and met.[19]

In a school where rje has been embraced, there are concrete action steps that seek to address issues of implicit bias and discrimination.[20]

Concrete Action Steps to Support Just and Equitable Learning Environments

Return to the thinking box at the beginning of this chapter and consider the words and images you equated with justice and equity. Have those images changed after reading this chapter? The images we use to portray justice and equity will impact the types of decisions we make in schools. The desire to create more just and equitable schools must be accompanied by actions. Here are two areas where concrete steps can be taken.

Culturally Inclusive Pedagogy

One way to think about supporting justice and equity is in decisions about curriculum and instruction. As noted earlier, a great number of resources for educators are related to culturally responsive pedagogy.[21] In rje schools, curricular decisions are made in ways that honor and respect all people regardless of their race, ethnicity, language, gender, sexual orientation, income, or ability. Here are some ideas:[22]

- When choosing textbooks, consider finding authors with diverse backgrounds and who bring a wide range of experiences.
- Ensure that literature for children and youth reflects the diversity of students in the school and features characters who look, talk, and live like them.
- Use resources and materials that consider historical harms and highlight the experiences of those who have been ignored. For example, history classes should not only address the ways in which Indigenous peoples were brutalized, but also highlight the contributions that they have made and continue to make. Additionally, as advocates of rje talk about a needs-based approach, let's be sure to tell the whole history about how Maslow's (and others') ideas were influenced by Indigenous people and that virtually all of educational psychology has ignored this history.
- Poetry and literature units should include writings from more than just white European authors.

Beyond materials and resources, the classroom environment also creates opportunities for promoting justice and equity. At times, teachers and administrators can overlook the gaps that exist between their own experiences and those of their students. Consider the following:

- Think about the *sample problems* used in math and science classes. Are they relevant to the lived experiences of all of our students, or do they make assumptions based on majority views? One science teacher intentionally references breakthroughs made by women in STEM (science, technology, engineering, and math) fields in order to promote gender equity.

- Think about the *words we use*. How easily teachers can perpetuate assumptions about marriage and relationships without considering that some children live with aunts or uncles, two moms, or foster parents. One teacher in Virginia refers to students' "grown-ups" rather than their parents in an effort to be more inclusive about possible family configurations.

- Think about *equity issues* related to religious diversity. If you celebrate the religious holidays of one group of students, then the holidays of all students should be celebrated. Putting up a Christmas tree and singing Christmas carols is appropriate, as long as other students, like Kali at the beginning of this chapter, are also invited to share and

Many rje practitioners, such as Anita Wadhwa of the Restorative Justice Collaborative of Houston, are equipping students to facilitate circle processes. How might you work to ensure that students are more involved in leading the rje work at your school?

have their holiday traditions honored. In an rje classroom, for example, the third-grade teacher might also have other winter celebrations represented in the class decorations, or students might sit in a circle together and share stories with the class about their various holiday traditions.

Full Participation for All Members of the Community

Another way to consider justice and equity in schools and classrooms is to ensure that all members of the community can participate fully in school-related events and activities. Students who feel marginalized are often disconnected from learning and from social interaction. They are often underrepresented in advanced placement classes, overrepresented in remedial classes, less likely to be recognized for their accomplishments, and more likely to drop out of school. One concrete thing schools can do is complete an internal equity audit and then make policy decisions that promote justice and equity.

One way that rje promotes full participation is with students requiring special education services. Research suggests that students with special needs are suspended or expelled at disproportionately higher rates than non-identified students. To counter this, special educators like Leila Peterson[23] and Julie Camerata[24] are working to blend rje and special education in ways that reduce exclusionary discipline for students with special needs and that ensure that their instructional needs are fully met. In addition, Peterson and Camerata promote full participation by creating spaces where students receiving special education services are invited to participate in their annual IEP (individualized education program) meetings and to give input on instructional decisions.[25]

Within rje, equitable participation is not limited to students. When meetings occur, all who have a stake in the decisions being made should be invited so that their voices are heard. For example, invite cafeteria and custodial staff to give input on school-related decisions. Include teachers in decisions about curriculum and instruction. Place a priority on the involvement of parents, caregivers, and family members of students as essential members of the learning community.

Summary

Rje leads us to focus on the worth, well-being, and relational essence of being human. There is a deliberate shift away from individualism toward interconnectedness, treating one another with justice and equity.

Chapter 5:
Nurturing Healthy
Relationships

Take 3–5 minutes to draw a mind map of the relationships you encounter and impact in one day; you can use pictures and/or words. Begin by putting yourself in the center of the page. From here, make a web that identifies each of the people you have direct contact with in a regular school day. Next, add the names of all the places where you work and live. Finally, add a word or two to each of these that describe your feelings when you are relating with these people and places.

The quantity, complexity, and reach of relationships that occur in a school are mind-boggling. When educators' beliefs and values align with those of restorative justice in education (rje), relationships become evident wherever we look, as does the realization that their quality shapes the school's culture, students' ability to learn, and everyone's ability to thrive in the educational environment. Thus, nurturing healthy relationships is an essential element for just and equitable learning environments, as well as for addressing harm and conflict.

Three stories illustrate the comprehensiveness of relationships and how they are nurtured—from the interpersonal to the social, from the more obvious to the subtle:

- Simone dreads going to the meetings where she sits with a group of "experts" to discuss what is best for each of her children in terms of educational programming. Her kids both have learning needs that can't be met in the regular classroom. She feels intimidated as she sits at the end of a table with the guidance counselor, special education teacher, school psychologist, and a school administrator. They always invite her to share her ideas for what she thinks might be best. She wonders why they ask; they never take her suggestions seriously, and usually have the plan printed off for her to sign when she arrives. Will today's meeting be different? The administrator called and told her they were using a different approach where they would write the plan at the meeting and also invited her to take a friend or relative along if she wished. She's not sure what will happen, but is glad her best friend and her children's godparent, Alyx has agreed to come.
- Ken is struck by the messages inherent in the math curriculum. Eager for his students to understand the world of finance for personal and social well-being, he reads the problem-solving activities and discovers

a repeated emphasis on the "buying power" of the individual with little regard for addressing the concerns of people marginalized by poverty. He begins to revise the learning activities to honor the worth and interconnectedness of all people.

- Trevor goes to the office to pick up a late slip before going to his first-grade class. He stands on his tiptoes to ring the bell on the counter. He waits quietly until he hears a voice asking him what he needs. After he leaves, Ms. Cortes wonders how she would feel if she were Trevor. She is glad that plans are being made to redesign the office spaces to be more child-friendly.

The Challenge of the Current Context

Nurturing and maintaining healthy relationships is not a subject taught in schools. There may be the occasional health unit highlighting what relationship is and educators may work with students when arguments and fights detract from learning curriculum content. In a similar way, learning how to breathe has rarely been a part of schooling unless it relates to playing a wind instrument, running a race, or winding down after a time of activity. Neither breathing nor relationships have had focused attention in the field of education.

Until recently.

In the 2016 edition, we identified that the challenge of our current education context was showing up as disconnection, feelings of isolation, and a lack of belonging. We said, "breathing" is becoming labored, painful, and shallow because the inherent need to belong has been undermined. The results include growing levels of anxiety and other diagnoses of mental illness, escalating interpersonal and social conflicts, high student and educator dropout rates, and ongoing school suspensions and expulsions. Educators are noting and struggling to respond to increasing needs, and recent research identifies diagnoses of toxic stress for growing numbers of children and youth from all sociocultural contexts who struggle to bond and build trust with parents, teachers, and/or guardians. These caregivers, often in spite of good intentions, are themselves disconnected and preoccupied, caught in hectic lifestyles without the knowledge or means for meeting the needs of their children.[1]

Since then, the analogy of "breathing" has taken on significantly deeper meaning—from a virus that attacks the lungs, to the thick smoke that covers much of the globe due to summer fires making it nearly impossible to breathe, to the chokeholds that impede the breathing of Black men, to escalating wars that destroy the breathing capacity of hundreds of thousands of people. Along with these physical restrictions for breathing, anxiety, conflict, and toxic stress have also multiplied. In educational contexts, we are turning our attention to the physical realities of breathing conditions and we are turning our attention to civic, social, and interpersonal relationships. What we had once taken for granted is draining away before us. And many of us have no concept for how to proceed with hope.

Though not the complete answer, rje does hold significant potential for addressing both the threat to our physical breathing and the threat to our ability to be in right relationship with each other. Core to rje are healthy relationships characterized by attachment and belonging. In a world where we have been encouraged and "educated" to believe that success is tied to individual effort and increasing wealth, rje confronts this way of being and thinking by uniquely emphasizing people's connection to and dependence on one another, not their independence; rje exposes the underbelly of competition and standardized testing by uniquely emphasizing cooperation, collaboration, and the worth of every living being regardless of their productivity.

And rje supports and expects that experiencing; learning about and understanding what constitutes quality relationships that are mutually beneficial and interdependent is explicit and central to everyone's knowledge.

Rje is a significant response to a disconnected society. Healthy relationships, characterized by attachment and belonging, are a critical element for well-being. Rje uniquely emphasizes people's *dependence* on one another, not their independence. For relationships to become mutually beneficial, or *interdependent*, it is necessary to be aware of what constitutes quality relationships.

Identifying Quality Relationships

Healthy relationships are nurtured when people communicate respectfully and share power in a way that allows for individual and collective needs to be met. Respectful communication occurs when people take into account the reality that the messages they send and receive will have an impact on others' sense of worth and well-being. It encourages people to be at their best even in challenging circumstances. This is possible when people recognize the role power plays. Inherently, power is neither good nor bad. How power is used will impact the health of relationships.[2] When power is employed in self-serving ways, relationships are diminished because others are used as objects to further the well-being or success of self. The questions introduced in Chapter 3—*Am I measuring? Am I honoring? What message am I sending?*—help uncover the impact of power in relationship. If I measure others, I send messages that there is an imbalance of power and one of us has *power over* the other. If I honor others, I send messages that I am willing to share *power with* you. If I consciously consider what messages I send when I communicate, I am alert to the possibility of power imbalance.

Educational institutions have been designed to be hierarchical. People in schools often experience or engage with power in unbalanced ways. When people feel they are required to submit to another's power, it is common for them to push back and exert their own power either subtly or overtly. They might also simply comply with the stronger power and negate their own worth. Because every action results in interaction, rje works to ensure that power is employed in a manner that nurtures well-being. The Relationship Matrix[3] (Figure 5.1) illustrates this.

Power is embodied in the *support* and *expectations* that people have for one another's humanity (their worth and interconnectedness) as identified on the horizontal and vertical axes. When people provide support and expectations in a balanced, reciprocal

73

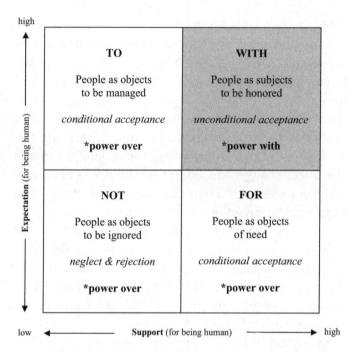

Figure 5.1: Relationship Matrix (power over; power with).

way, power is used constructively, is available to all involved, and results in people engaging *with* each other. However, power becomes destructive in relationships if one sees it as a limited and desirable commodity. Because everyone needs to belong, doing what is necessary to belong then becomes competitive. Those who feel powerless will do whatever is necessary to gain control, find acceptance, or retreat, while those in power will do whatever necessary to maintain their position. In either situation, *power-over* relationships result in people doing things *to* or *for* each other, or more profoundly, ignoring each other completely (*not*).

74

The Relationship Matrix helps identify how we are in relationship with others. When relationships are new or become conflicted, the matrix can reveal gaps in support or expectations. Using it to assess strong relationships can reveal how support and expectations can be provided in balanced ways. When relationships are unbalanced, people become objects for the benefit of others. When they are balanced, relationships radiate respect, dignity, and mutual concern for each other.

Applying the Relationship Matrix

How can the Relationship Matrix be applied? Consider the following examples:

- *WITH:* Chris, a fourth-grade teacher, recognizes that she is in a position of power as an educator and that she could be using power to diminish or nurture the worth of a student, colleague, or parent. As a teacher engaged in rje, she aims to provide high support and high expectations. She works *with* her students so teaching and learning is reciprocal. When her class is repeatedly off-task on an assignment and she is unable to identify why, she calls her students to a talking circle meeting (described later) where each one is invited to respond to this question: "What is happening that makes it difficult to focus?" They share that the current assignment is too similar to one done in a previous grade. Chris is impressed with their ideas when she asks, "What should we do about this?" Then together they make a plan and adapt the unit. By *honoring* them as growing human beings and responding to

75

their circumstances, Chris holds them accountable to their responsibility in a supportive, collaborative manner. She does not attempt to control but instead engages them.

- *TO:* Chris also knows what it feels like to do things *to* her students and is uncomfortable with those memories. During the previous week, she kept two students in at recess to complete their work and then went to the staff room for coffee. She was too tired and frustrated to ask them what was happening that they couldn't finish their assignment in the time allotted. She also recalls the rewards charts that she publicly put stickers on for students working productively, embarrassing those students who were struggling to keep up. In both cases, her expectations exceeded her willingness to provide support. She is often tempted to use *power over* students to control their actions. When her students conform, it makes her look good. Teaching would be so much easier if the students were robots who did what they were programmed to do!

- *FOR:* Chris also recalls times when she provided high support but set low expectations for students. Because parents in prominent jobs intimidated her, she catered to the needs of their children. When they came late regularly or didn't contribute in class, she used her power to do things *for* them. She accepted their excuses readily, worked with them until they were done with their work, and communicated in a friendly manner with them. Chris knows now that she tried to be their friend and was using them for her benefit. When she is honest with herself, she admits far less patience for students in foster care or with parents on social assistance.

- *NOT:* Chris also knows what it is to *not* engage with her students. One year she was exhausted and burned out. It took all her energy just to show up for work. She has little memory of those students and realizes that she provided very little support or expectations for them. She created activities that were overly simple so she could sit at her desk while they worked. She was in survival mode and really needed help herself.

Chris's experience illustrates how it is possible for one person to engage with all four of the quadrants depending on the circumstances. Though the descriptions are straightforward to demonstrate the process of critical reflection, the reality often feels more complex. Sharing power in a balanced way can be difficult because relationships are always changing. The resulting growth, however, is beautiful as illustrated in the first example, where Chris shared *power with* the students who gained self-confidence. They realized that their perspectives were important!

> Think of times when you have engaged in relationships that would fit each of the four quadrants. What do you notice?

How RJE Understands and Supports Healthy Relationships in Education

Rje is primarily a means for changing self, not a means for changing others.[4] This separates rje from programs and approaches that have changing the behavior of children and youth as their goal. The focus on self may be surprising if educators believe that changing behavior is a key task for education. However, stemming from the belief that people are worthy and interconnected, restorative educators do not manage or control their students, but they become facilitators who create space and opportunities where students can engage.[5] In this way, rje creates invitational opportunities in which engagement, rather than control, is encouraged.

Listen for the phrases *classroom management, classroom control,* or *behavior management* in your particular context. Ask the following: What is the intention of this terminology? Does it encourage you to *engage* with your students or *control* them?

Recognizing that change begins with self, Ripples of Relationship (Figure 5.2)[6] illustrate the scope of an educator's interconnectedness in the school context. Rje begins with adults living in supportive relationships that create cultures where everyone—including children, youth, and other vulnerable populations—are honored as worthy, contributing members. Similar diagrams could be created from the point of view of students, caregivers, other support personnel, or broader community members.

Ripples of Relationship begin with a pebble thrown into water. All of our relationships are impacted by our conscious or unconscious beliefs and values. These are stable until our interactions with self and others disrupt our well-being or the well-being of others. When disruption happens, we often rethink or recommit to what we believe and value. Thus, the ripples reverberate outward from the center, but they can also be reversed as various encounters occur. We are individuals within a relational context where we impact and are impacted by those around us.

Out of core beliefs and values, our relationship *with self* is impacted—a relationship that is often

Figure 5.2: Ripples of Relationship

ignored or assumed. When we know ourselves well, our responses to others are more likely to be guided by a balance of support and expectations. Positive self-esteem and self-image are crucial. Yet when they are encouraged apart from a belief that all are worthy and relational, individualism and narcissism can result and undermine meaningful relationships. Rje affirms that in order to nurture interconnectedness, we need to see ourselves as valued, contributing parts of relationships. For some of us, it is easier to be self-deprecating than self-appreciating for various reasons. When this happens, our interactions with others are negatively impacted. We might refrain from contributing actively, contribute in a way that undermines others, or contribute to boost our own egos. Similar concerns arise when we value ourselves more than others.

Next, our relationships *with adults* are identified. School climates are heavily influenced by how adults relate to each other. If we can engage with our

> A person with Ubuntu is open and available to others, affirming of others, does not feel threatened that others are able and good, for he or she has a proper self-assurance that comes from knowing that he or she belongs in a greater whole and is diminished when others are humiliated or diminished.
> —Desmond Tutu, 1999

peers and colleagues authentically, we model for children and youth respect, dignity, and mutual concern. However, because of our innate need to belong, it can be difficult to support and encourage accountability for our peers if we fear rejection. It takes courage, confidence, and skill to address difficulty, as avoidance might seem easier.

If we relate well with peers and ourselves, we will more likely engage well *with students.* Because we are in authoritative, guiding roles with children and youth, (i.e., "bigger" than them), it is easy to slip into using *power over* them. By engaging *with* them with the same level of respect, dignity, and mutual concern we have for self and adults, we enter into relationships where we seek their well-being first.

> What happens to the respect offered to substitute teachers when they are called "guest teachers" instead? What happens when you take a moment to ask the custodian how they are?

As educators, we can be most effective in supporting students in their relationships with their peers and other adults when our relationships are healthy. Looking at *relationships among students,* as authority figures it is easy to slip into thinking that we can identify their issues and "fix it" for them. When we recognize our own shortcomings and realize how challenging our own interactions can be, we are more likely to walk *with* our students in their relationships, listening carefully so we can support them and encourage accountability.

As our awareness of relationships increases, we pay closer attention to the messages we send through *the curriculum content and pedagogy.* We realize that who or what we include or omit in terms of content has serious implications for students' perceptions of others. Curriculum and pedagogy will shape how students learn to relate to each other and their communities.

Next, our *relationship with the institution* is also impacted. The physical entity, the governing structures, the policies, and the procedures of a school have all been put in place and administered by groups of adults with a common goal. Sometimes that goal was well-meaning; other times the goal was motivated by an intentional desire to control (e.g., colonialism, white supremacy, segregation). Over time, even when the visions, missions, and mandates of institutions intend to share power, they can become vague or distorted. Hierarchical power dynamics are then more likely to take over and control rather than engage their constituents.

Finally, the core belief that all people are worthy and interconnected also has direct repercussions for our relationship with the natural environment all around us. In this era where we are becoming alert to climate change and the devastation human beings have caused for much of the planet and its resources, we realize how significant it is to recognize the reciprocal relationship we have with all things natural (air, water, land, animals, plants, etc.). Indigenous peoples around the globe have resiliently clung to this understanding, often animating these elements by calling

82

them "water people," "rock people," "tree people," "bird people,"[7] and showing those of us who are not Indigenous that respecting these parts of the created order opens our eyes to our dependence on these complex components of the world we live in. When we honor ourselves as worthy and interconnected, this will always extend to all that keep us alive.

Regardless of our roles in a school, as adults we recognize that we can contribute positively or negatively to how the school functions by remembering that bureaucracies are created by people. If they are found to be lacking in any way, people are needed to change them. It is easy to measure and blame "the system" when things go wrong. However, when we are engaged with "the system," we can honor it by advocating for change so the well-being of all becomes central.

Ripples of Relationship (Figure 5.2) identify the range of relationships that exist in educational contexts. Though each is presented as separate, in its own ring, the reality is much more complex as the relationships intersect, overlap, grow, and change, constantly influencing one another. By presenting school culture as a series of ripples, rje emphasizes the need for a clear understanding of how school relationships are nurtured.

Concrete Action Steps for Nurturing Healthy Relationships

In order to nurture healthy relationships, rje draws on comprehensive resources available and grounded in other theories (e.g., care theory, social-emotional learning [SEL], learning ecologies, etc.). However, any approach, rje included, can cause further harm when those involved are unaware of their personal core beliefs and values, or of those of the approach being used. The language of relationships can be prominent, but authentic relationships are easily co-opted by institutional expectations or self-interest. Thus, the first action step for nurturing healthy relationships has been the focus of this book—the awareness, acceptance, articulation, and enacting of core beliefs and values that uphold the interconnectedness, worth, and well-being of all.

Building on an analysis of core beliefs and values, two approaches—talking circles and learning to listen/learning to ask—are particularly relevant for encouraging the growth of relational school cultures. We hope that these approaches will open the way for recognizing the myriad other ways that healthy relationships can be encouraged.

Talking Circles

Talking circles, originating from various Indigenous cultures, are intentional spaces where the core beliefs and values of rje are practiced, experienced, and embodied.

Physically, a group sits in a circle and, with the guidance of a facilitator or "circle keeper," discusses agreed-upon topics in a manner that gives each person an opportunity to share. An object of meaning for the group (e.g., a stone, a plant, a stuffed toy, etc.), usually referred to as a "talking piece," is passed from person to person around the circle to indicate who holds the space. People are invited to share, pass, or hold a time of silence when the piece comes to them.

The circle, which has no beginning or end, symbolically illustrates that all present are valued as significant and that insights shared are held respectfully within that space.

A facilitator or circle keeper's roles can include inviting people to attend, setting up the space, opening the time, introducing dialogue guidelines, presenting the topic, keeping the conversation focused, and closing the circle.

Though the process appears to be simple and is actually simple enough for even young children to facilitate for their peers, it is also intricately complex. Carolyn Boyes-Watson and Kay Pranis articulate how circle dialogues are much more than just putting chairs in a circle: "We are practicing basic ways that are fundamental to being successful together."[8] Within a circle, individual and collective ideas and needs are brought into one space. By giving people a designated opportunity to hear and be heard, trust develops. Over time, this trust and practice in listening and speaking transfers to relationships away from the circle, positively impacting the ways people relate to one another.

In a school setting, talking circles can take on various formats:

- Talking circles can be very quick, short, and lighthearted as a way of getting to know more about each other and acknowledging each other's presence (e.g., staff meetings, classroom meetings, committee meetings).
- Talking circles can provide time for adults to contribute perspectives about their responsibilities at

a meeting or for students to contribute ideas about academic work or social concerns.

- Talking circles can be held at the end of a meeting, a lesson, a day, or a week when everyone shares a question they are left with, one thing they have learned, or something they will do before the next gathering.
- Talking circles can be classroom meetings that provide an opportunity for everyone to contribute about how they experienced the past week and what they need for the coming week.
- Talking circles can explore in-depth curricular topics such as race, privilege, or climate change.
- Talking circles can be spaces to process grief when a peer or colleague dies.
- Talking circles can provide opportunities to address serious harm caused between individuals or the group as a whole.
- Talking circles can be used to gather information for individualized education programs (IEPs) so all contributors with insight into a student's needs have a clear voice (this can also include the student).

A growing variety of resources are available to support learning how to facilitate talking circles (see page 84). However, in-person professional development will help you grasp the nuances involved. It's important to note that facilitating for serious harm is challenging and requires significant training and support. Be aware that further harm can be done if facilitated without proper preparation.

In essence, when talking circles become a key form of communication in classrooms and schools, the culture becomes one in which all are honored as worthy and interconnected.

Learning to Listen and Learning to Ask

To communicate effectively, knowing what we "should" do is not enough. It takes practice to learn *how* to listen for understanding, rather than for replying, and *how* to ask open-ended questions that generate authentic dialogue. Open-ended questions can help critically reflect on what is happening around us. Five key questions suggested in a variety of restorative justice (rj) literature include the following:

- *What happened/is happening?*
- *What was/am I feeling/thinking?*
- *What is the hardest/best thing for me?*
- *Who is impacted by this? How?*
- *What do I need [to do] to move forward?*

These questions can deepen learning, address challenging situations, or be used to explore harmful situations. The responses to these questions tell a story of past, present, and future. In a group context, hearing the responses of others highlights the importance of different perspectives. On our own, the questions encourage us to dig below the obvious.

Three examples illustrate how the questions can be used in very different contexts:

- During a math lesson on probability, Mr. Blake uses a checkup circle. He gathers small groups for five minutes and invites students to respond to one or more of the five key questions. Mr. Blake notices that the students who grasp the concepts share the steps of how they got their answers and then stretch their thinking into life applications. He notices that students who are more uncertain or confused articulate where they are stuck. Some identify the spot where they require support from others. He notices how the lesson becomes relational as the students engage with one another's thinking instead of relying on his expertise or the need for a right or wrong answer.

- As Ms. Slade begins to plan for a new unit, she finds herself confused and overwhelmed by the task. She stops and takes five minutes to go for a walk. As she walks, she talks aloud to herself and answers the key questions. By the time she returns, she realizes that she is unclear about the purpose of the unit and feels that her students with learning challenges will be lost. She digs into the curriculum documents for more detail and then stops to talk to her colleague who had taught this class the previous year. Before she heads home, a plan forward is taking shape.

- Ms. Polet used to struggle to engage in conversations with parents and caregivers. Now she finds herself looking forward to phone calls home, beginning conversations with relational questions such as, "How was your day today?" or "What has been life-giving for you recently?" She is always struck by how much more students' grown-ups open up, which allows her to have more generative conversations about what is happening with their children in her classes.

Learning to listen and to ask questions is critical for nurturing relationships. Listening carefully will guide how and what we ask, and how or what we ask will guide our listening. The dialogue that results opens up opportunities for us to turn core beliefs and values into practice.

Summary

Nurturing healthy relationships is a key component of restorative justice in education. When combined with just and equitable learning environments, the setting is well prepared to address situations in which people are in conflict or cause each other significant harm. In Chapter 6 we discuss repairing harm and transforming conflict.

Chapter 6:
Repairing Harm and Transforming Conflict

Think about a time when you experienced harm.
In that moment, what did you need from others?
List some ideas. Now think about a time when you
caused someone else harm. In that moment, what
did you need from others? List some ideas. Look
at your lists. What do you notice? Are you meeting
these needs for your students? Your colleagues?
Yourself?

Given the primacy of relationships for restorative justice in education (rje) initiatives in schools, it is crucial that we nurture those relationships and work toward healing when they are compromised. Our best intentions and efforts at nurturing healthy relationships can still result in conflict and harm. That harm leaves us with unmet needs—for repair, for hope, for autonomy, for belonging. We are able to nurture our relationships in healthy ways when we consider what we need and what others need when relationships break down.

Consider the following situations:

- Jolee sat in the bathroom and stared at the mirror, wishing that she could make herself look more like the other girls in her class. Tears streamed down her face as she recalled their unkind words, relentless and harsh. They teased her all the time and no one, not even her teacher, ever stopped them. It seemed that there was no one who would stick up for her and no one to turn to for help.

- Braden had been in in-school suspension (ISS) for forty-eight days this school year. Most were due to office referrals from his science teacher, Mr. Marks. Braden felt that Mr. Marks seemed to look for ways to get him in trouble. Braden didn't understand why Mr. Marks hated him so much and why everything he did in Mr. Marks's class was wrong.

- Mr. Marks worked tirelessly to provide engaging instructional activities for his students. Most seemed to appreciate the effort and occasionally expressed gratitude for being such a caring teacher. Braden, however, was different. Mr. Marks felt that Braden seldom participated and seemed to look for ways to get out of doing any work. Mr. Marks didn't understand why Braden hated him so much and why he refused to engage with science.

The preceding vignettes highlight the complicated nature of relationships and invite us to think about what is needed in each situation for healing and transformation to occur.

Defining Harm and Conflict

Harm is more than a physical or emotional injury. It is anything that undermines a person's dignity or minimizes their worth. Harm doesn't have to be intentional. We might cause harm with what we deem to be innocent comments or actions. Additionally, people can experience harm because of institutional policies and practices or because of cultural norms. As Fania Davis articulates in her *Little Book of Race and Restorative Justice*, harms, like racism, can show up at the individual, institutional, and structural levels and include not only interpersonal harms, but also historical harms, such as genocide and slavery.

Likewise, *conflict* is more than simply two people disagreeing. Conflict is a relational interaction. When we engage in conflict, we acknowledge that relationship. We might disagree with someone, but if we don't acknowledge a relationship with the person (i.e., we don't share a mutual concern for one another), it remains a disagreement but not necessarily a conflict. Conflict emerges within relationships when the disagreement has potential implications for the relationship.

The examples of Braden and Mr. Marks illustrate the possibility that both the teacher and the student are experiencing harm. Every time Braden is sent to ISS, it confirms his belief that Mr. Marks is out to get him. It feels like a personal attack on his dignity, perpetuating his sense of injustice and decreasing the likelihood that he will be engaged in science class. Conversely, every time Braden disengages in class, it sends a message to Mr. Marks that Braden doesn't care about learning science. The teacher might take it personally, perceiving it as an attack on his dignity.

Students and teachers alike may go to great extremes to protect their sense of dignity and avoid feeling harmed by the other. Students may lash out at teachers or avoid going to class. Teachers may ignore students or work harder to find ways to exclude them through suspension or expulsion. What if these cycles could be transformed into relationships of mutual concern?

A Word about School Discipline and Student Behavior

This chapter is about harm and conflict, not about student behavior. Even within rje approaches, too often the focus is limited to "fixing" student behavior while ignoring the context from which that behavior emerges. Think about the image we began the book with: when a flower is not blooming in a garden, we don't automatically blame the flower. For example, we see a student lash out at a teacher with angry words or disrespect and we name that *misbehavior*. Defining it as *misbehavior* allows us to consider the action apart from its context. From an rje perspective, angry words or disrespect are externalized *responses*. Behavior comes from some place—it has a context. It's possible that the student is academically frustrated and feels embarrassed about their lack of ability. It could be that the teacher inadvertently said something that the student felt was insulting. The possibilities are endless. Rje assumes that there are reasons for students' responses and intentionally creates spaces to uncover those reasons. Simply addressing student behavior without addressing the context will ultimately fail.

93

Rje moves the focus beyond incidents to the context. The incident is important because it opens doors for us to consider the health of the context, but if all we do is address the incident, we aren't truly addressing harm.

Several great books about addressing school discipline through a contextual lens have been written. For example, *The Little Book of Restorative Discipline for Schools,* by Lorraine Stutzman Amstutz and Judy Mullet, provides a thorough treatment of restorative discipline as an alternative to punitive approaches for addressing student behavior, while concurrently acknowledging the importance of changing school culture. (For additional resources, see page 125.)

Understanding Harm

In contrast to the current legal system, restorative justice (rj) defines crime and conflict as a "violation of people and relationships" rather than a violation of rules or laws. Rj seeks to ask a different set of questions. Rather than who broke a rule and what punishments does the person deserve, rj asks who was harmed, what needs are present because of the harm, and who is obligated to meet those needs.[1]

In schools and classrooms, we too often overlook harms that are not explicitly written in the discipline codes. For example, consider Zach's experience in school. Due to thick glasses that enable him to read better, Zach had been teased since he started middle school. When he decided that he'd had enough and pushed another student, he was suspended for five days for violating the discipline code. But isn't the teasing he had received also a "violation of people

94

and relationships"? Shouldn't it be considered a form of harm? In an rje setting, the harms, needs, and obligations of each person engaged in the situation would be addressed, creating a more just outcome for all involved.

Harm also extends beyond interpersonal relationships. For example, Billy has difficulty reading, but due to restrictions about the number of students who can be served in special education, he does not qualify. Each day, he enters school without a strong enough foundation in reading to be able to access the curriculum. One day, his history teacher, Mr. Omari, becomes frustrated with him for not being able to complete assignments independently. Sensing Mr. Omari's frustration, Billy yells at him, is sent to the office, and ultimately is suspended for three days. In this situation, who experienced harm? Whose dignity was violated? Who is responsible for creating harm? What responsibility does the system hold for causing harm? How does this incident highlight structural injustices that need to be addressed?

What harm do other systemic policies—such as an excessive reliance on standardized testing, English-only immersion policies for English Language Learners (ELLs), and zero tolerance policies— cause to teachers, students, and families?

> We have all experienced harm at the hands of "the system." Think about a time when the source of your own pain wasn't a person but something more structural.

95

As we discuss in Chapter 2, the early 1990s brought about zero tolerance policies that served to impose mandatory suspensions for specific behaviors. Not only are zero tolerance policies ineffective, but in many cases they also actually perpetuate the behaviors they are intending to stop because they further harm the one suspended. Students who are excluded from school fall behind academically. They are often labeled or treated with less respect. Feelings of injustice serve to deepen students' loss of dignity, often increasing their defiance toward authority figures.

Citing Carol Gilligan, Howard Zehr notes that those who are considered "offenders" are often those who have experienced injustice. Their behaviors can be seen as an attempt to correct injustice.[2] We are not attempting to excuse their behaviors; rather, we want to understand "what happened" to influence their choices. Unless we address underlying injustices—providing opportunities for them to be included in an rj process, for example—we may end up reinforcing their sense of injustice. According to Ronnie Casella, some students are able to "bounce back from a suspension or expulsion," but students "who are already negatively affected by poverty, racism, academic failure, and other realities" experience such punishment differently—they often struggle to recover.[3] In a report on the impact of zero tolerance policies, the American Psychological Association concluded that these policies fail to make schools safer and run "counter to our best knowledge of child development."[4] Sometimes our policies can cause harm.

Trauma, stress, and poverty can also create cycles of harm in school settings that lead to decreased feelings of safety and security, impacting learning, relationships, and the school climate. For example, according to research on adverse childhood experiences (ACEs),[5] students who experience high ACE scores often miss a great deal of school, have trouble maintaining focus, and exhibit impulsive behaviors.

> In what ways has trauma impacted your own life? Take some time to read up on trauma and consider ways your school might create a more trauma-informed school culture.

Violent and defiant behaviors are symptoms of trauma and other injustices. In *The Little Book of Trauma Healing,* Carolyn Yoder notes that the impact of trauma can range from *acting-in* behaviors, such as substance abuse or suicide, to *acting-out* behaviors, such as aggressive behaviors or high-risk activities. Other signs of trauma include apathy, lack of empathy, or impaired communication.[6] Research is emerging that suggests that the effects of historical trauma (e.g., residential schools, slavery, genocide) can be passed along genetically to future generations.[7]

The good news is that research also indicates that the negative impact of trauma can be offset by the care and support of a significant adult. When we create caring places where students' needs are met, there is hope for the restoration of relationships as well as the restoration of dignity, a sense of self, and resiliency. The documentary *Paper Tigers,* for example, traced the transformation of one high school that recognized the impact that trauma, conflict, and stress had on students. Implementing a trauma-informed approach, the school noted fewer office referrals and suspensions, fewer fights, an increase in the graduation rate, an increase in test scores, and an increase in college acceptance among graduates.[8]

Understanding Conflict

Like harm, much has been written about conflict in educational settings. The fields of conflict resolution education and peer mediation have helped transform many conflicts. Rje provides another dimension. Schools that adopt rje should consider the role that dignity plays in nurturing healthy relationships. The goal is to work with conflict in ways that strengthen an individual's sense of dignity.

Conflict is inevitable within any relationship where there is a sense of mutual concern for another. When conflict emerges, the tendency is to seek a resolution.

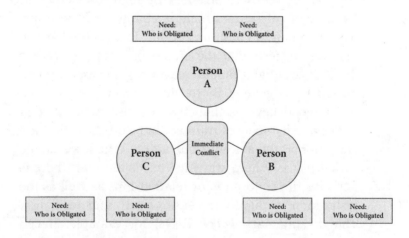

Figure 6.1: Conflict Exercise

98

Professional development for conflict management or conflict resolution in schools is important. Many students (and arguably, many educators) are not equipped with the skills to work through conflict in ways that create peaceable outcomes.

Try this exercise: Think about an incident where there was conflict. Who were the people involved in that incident? Who experienced harm? Create a diagram like the one in Figure 6.1. Include a circle for each person impacted by the conflict. Then out from each circle, consider what needs are represented by the harm they have experienced. Beside each need, identify who might be able or obligated to meet that need. This type of analysis begins to help us see that conflict is complex and relational.

The way people respond to conflict can either strengthen or harm relationships. Positive outcomes of conflict depend on whether we are able to maintain our dignity in the midst of the conflict. As noted in Chapter 3, dignity is related to our sense of worth. According to Donna Hicks, an international affairs facilitator, our sense of dignity can be disrupted when we are in conflict, leaving us feeling vulnerable, out of control, or worthless. By creating spaces for addressing conflict in ways that restore dignity, we not only resolve the conflict but also potentially transform it into something healing. Conflict, in and of itself, is not detrimental to relationships; conflict that disrupts our sense of dignity is.[9]

Hicks differentiates between dignity and respect. Dignity, she states, is a birthright, inherent in our humanity. We might talk about someone needing to earn respect, but dignity cannot and does not have to be earned; it just is. As with trauma, when our dignity is threatened, we can become irrational in our attempts at survival and self-preservation. This can often lead us to retreat from a situation or to lash out at the threat, creating a cycle of harm. We often see these responses in students (and teachers) who experience conflict as an attack on their dignity.

Dignity is about value, honor, and worth. When we treat others with dignity, we recognize their humanity. That, in and of itself, can be healing for some. When we are treated with dignity, we are able to connect with others in healthy ways, thrive in our academic settings, and talk rationally about conflicts—leading to better outcomes. In the next section, we discuss ways that rje specifically addresses issues of harm and conflict.

How RJE Addresses Harm and Conflict

Howard Zehr defines rj as "a process to involve, to the extent possible, those who have a stake in a specific offense and to collectively identify and address harms, needs, and obligations, in order to heal and put things as right as possible."[10] Acknowledging the importance of providing a "guide to how we live together day by day" in schools, Lorraine Stutzman Amstutz and Judy Mullet add this definition:

[Rj] promotes values and principles that use inclusive, collaborative approaches for being in community. These approaches validate the experiences and needs of everyone within the community, particularly those who have been marginalized, oppressed, or harmed. These approaches allow us to act and respond in ways that are healing rather than alienating or coercive.[11]

Thus, when we embrace rje, we are more concerned with people getting what they need for healing and justice than about what they deserve. As we consider how rje helps us address harm and conflict, a primary principle is a focus on underlying needs.

Addressing the Needs of All Involved

Rj emerged in response to a criminal justice system where too often the needs of those who have been harmed are ignored as the system takes on the role of victim. The same thing often happens in schools. Policies are designed to punish the student who breaks the rules, without considering the needs of the person, or people, who are impacted by conflict or harm. Rje seeks to ensure that when harm occurs, the needs of those who have been impacted are met in ways that restore what has been broken, whether that is their sense of self, a relationship, or the hope that the school environment is still a safe place for them.

Return to the conflict analysis diagram that you completed (Figure 6.1). Think about the needs that are represented by the harms. Some of those needs can and should be met in a classroom environment, while others cannot. Sometimes teachers and school personnel either are not equipped or do not have the resources to address the needs that students bring to school with them or that they experience at school. For example, a student with a high ACE score might need more than support from educators; they might need professional counseling as well. However, educators can and should play a role in helping students find and access appropriate supports by making referrals to service providers. A student who steals food because they are hungry does not need to be criminalized; rather educators can and should connect that student with services that address food insecurity.

At the core of repairing harms from an rje perspective is a concern for the needs of each person involved.

Making Things Right

Rje attempts to make things right to the extent possible. The goals are repairing what is broken and restoring what has been harmed. In some cases, making things right may be in the form of restitution. For example, if a student vandalizes a teacher's car out of anger and frustration, we want to find out the context—what was the student responding to? Another priority, however, is to make things right for the teacher. People who are harmed often feel disempowered. Giving them an opportunity to make decisions about repairing harm allows them to regain a sense of control. In the preceding example, if the teacher requested that the student work toward paying for the damaged vehicle, the physical damage, as well as an emotional need for stability, could be repaired.

In other cases, making things right is less clear. How do you repair trust that has been broken? How do we restore a sense of dignity that has been violated or someone's sense of worth? How do we make right years of inequitable educational opportunities for students who attend underfunded, underresourced schools? These are critical questions that can be answered only in the context of the community.

Dennis Sullivan and Larry Tifft argue that when people who have caused harm are given an opportunity to make things right, it creates the possibility for them to "transcend the script" of negative identity often attached to those who cause harm.[12] The opportunity to make things right is a more effective means of holding students accountable than merely punishing them.

Building Supportive Accountability

Rj has often been critiqued for being too soft and for letting students get away with disruptive behaviors. Opponents fear that without significant enough consequences for negative behaviors, chaos will result, ultimately interfering with learning. In reality, rj does emphasize accountability. However, in rje, accountability is not about being *held* accountable *for* certain behaviors, making the individual a passive recipient of someone else's decisions. Instead, rje promotes accountability *to* one's community, supporting people as they take responsibility through intentional actions that repair what was harmed or violated. Within an rje community, everyone is accountable to a shared set of expectations and to others within that community. Further, within an rje framework, accountability takes place within a supportive community, which allows those in the community to maintain their sense of belonging and dignity even when they have caused harm (refer to Figure 5.1).

Consider a situation in which other staff members overhear a teacher berating a colleague. There are often no formal rules against this type of behavior, so requiring that the teacher be held accountable for her words is unlikely. Within an rje community, however, there would be a place for acknowledging the berating as a violation of dignity and creating an opportunity for the teacher to demonstrate account-ability to an established faculty ethos of nurturing relationships. In addition, both teachers would have the opportunity through some type of restorative process, such as a talking circle, for receiving sup-port from other members of the teaching community while they worked through their conflict. To this end, rje moves beyond merely restoring relation-ships to transforming them. The Ontario Secondary School Teachers' Federation has been a leader in providing mediation services in exactly this arena. Its twelve mediators facilitate restorative dialogues with members experiencing conflict with other mem-bers. Established in 2001, the requests for restorative processes within this unique model grow every year. Anecdotal evidence is strong that when these meet-ings shift from solely "rights-based" to "relation-ship-based" interests, relationships become stronger through the process, and individuals report feeling a much better connection to their educational com-munities. The presenting issues that necessitated the mediation are addressed and do not reappear.

Transforming Conflict

Transforming conflict means addressing the immedi-ate situation and *at the same time* building capacity to strengthen relationships. Without conflict, needs may remain unmet and harm may go unacknowledged.

Returning to the analogy of the plant, biologists agree that wind and heavy rain that seem to be so destructive for a plant can actually serve to strengthen root and stem systems, therefore building resilience in the plant.

The transformative potential of conflict is consistent with some of our best understanding about how we learn. Jean Piaget, a developmental psychologist, built a theory of learning around the concepts of equilibrium and disequilibrium. Only when learners experience disequilibrium do they adapt and build new understanding or revise outdated ideas. In the same way, learning doesn't happen without the conflict of ideas. For example, Ben has experienced bullying by football players. He develops a perception of *all* football players as mean, violent, and aggressive. Jeffrey is on the football team and in Ben's fifth period class. Ben automatically dislikes Jeffrey. They experience conflict in class. Through an rje process, Ben adjusts his perception about football players. The conflict became an opportunity to learn.

> Think about a time when you experienced conflict and came through it stronger, wiser, or more resilient. Consider what enabled you to grow as a result of the conflict.

Likewise, John Dewey, a progressive educational philosopher, talked about the essential role that conflict plays in creating new ideas and ingenuity, claiming, "Conflict is the gadfly of thought . . . It shocks us out of sheep-like passivity."[13] Conflict doesn't always do this, he went on to say, but if we know that it can stir up new thoughts, we can embrace its transformative potential. Rje practitioners welcome conflict, believing that when we bring conflict to the fore, a community can work collaboratively to solve the problems *of* the community *within* the community.

Another way that rje transforms conflict is by creating opportunities to build social-emotional capacities, such as empathetic listening, self-regulation, problem solving, and perspective taking. In *The Little Book of Circle Processes,* Kay Pranis notes that being in talking circles together allows participants to articulate and practice their core beliefs and values. Values for nurturing relationships emerge, such as honoring another's perspective, listening respectfully, and speaking one's own truth. In our own experience, we have found circle processes to be a thriving place of transformation. In order for transformative experiences to happen, however, we need to return to our discussion of justice and equity.

Addressing Justice and Equity

Rje holds a deep commitment to creating just and equitable learning environments. Further, it resists hierarchical relationships that rely on *power over* rather than *power with*. Thus, another way that rje works to repair harm and transform conflict is by repairing those relationships that have been damaged by injustice. When educators feel, for example, that they have little choice in curriculum or instructional decisions, they may experience that lack of power as an injustice. Educators might seek to rectify that injustice by grasping at power over their students through what we call "trickle-down bullying."

Trickle-down bullying is a concept that implies that when someone in power over us uses that power in coercive ways, our tendency is to grasp for power from somewhere else. Sometimes that grasping for power comes at the expense of someone with less power than us. For example, school administrators may feel powerless in the face of so many regulations and grasp for power by placing pressure on teachers to get test scores up. Teachers, feeling a lack of empowerment, grab for power over their students, who then grasp for power over other students. Within this model, bullying becomes a structural phenomenon, one that we will likely not fix through bullying prevention programs. Rje seeks to restore a sense of agency to administrators, teachers, and students so that each experiences just and equitable relationships.

Within an rje framework, repairing harm and making things right are about restoring balance and a sense of harmony and justice. This will require addressing the injustices that marginalized groups have felt for generations. Oppression and injustice must be addressed if we are truly going to repair harm and transform conflict. In his essay on student resistance to learning, Herbert Kohl[14] differentiates between those students who *can't* learn and those who *won't* learn. For some students, the act of "not learning" is one way that they can push back against a system that they deem is unfair and unjust. Rje approaches will likely be ineffective until we develop a critical consciousness about the harmful impacts of

- racism,
- classism,
- sexism,
- homophobia,
- colonialism, and
- other forms of oppression.[15]

According to Denise Breton,[16] an author and the director of Living Justice Press, rj begins when those who have committed harms acknowledge their actions, take responsibility, and begin to work to make things right. Tracing the history of colonization that has characterized North America, she goes on to argue that it doesn't make sense to hold an Indigenous person "accountable for drug possession or stealing a car while we fail to hold ourselves [as settlers] accountable for genocide that we committed so we could steal an entire state's worth of land." In Edward Valandra's chapter in *Colorizing Restorative Justice*, we are reminded that one of the primary principles of rj is to "undo harm caused by wrongdoing." Valandra names the historical harm caused by settler colonialism as "the First Harm" and states plainly that it is doubtful that rj will "fulfill its promise as long as you [settlers] turn a blind eye to the one massive harm that predicates all the rest." If we are serious about rje, addressing historical harms and conflicts has to be part of our work.

Concrete Action Steps for Repairing Harm and Transforming Conflict

Being proactive in creating school climates where the well-being of *every* member is sought requires that rje facilitators return over and over to the core beliefs of interconnectedness, worth, and the well-being of all participants. The following are specific ways that schools can build on those beliefs and begin to move toward the potential of rje to repair harm and transform conflict.

Create Systems and Structures for Addressing Harm and Conflict

Creating structural supports for rje is one way to ensure that addressing harm and conflict becomes a part of the culture of a school. Many schools already have peer mediation programs, anti-bullying programs, or SEL (social-emotional learning) initiatives. These are great places to begin connecting the principles of rje to already existing structures. Ensuring that there is access to support resources—either on campus or through community-based providers—can help address individuals' needs. For example, one school designated an area of the school as a student support center. The counselors' offices, the nurse's office, and academic tutoring were all located there, making access to support easy for students. Students also knew that they could go to a small conference room there to work through conflicts. Trained rje volunteers staffed the student support center twice a week and were available to facilitate circles or conferences.

Rethink School Discipline Systems

School discipline systems should be redesigned in ways that are supportive of rje values and do not create further harm. Ongoing opportunities to participate in circle processes (i.e., circles of support and accountability, student conferencing, and reentry practices)can support students and adults who exhibit more challenging behaviors.

Suspensions and/or expulsions should be used only in extreme or severe situations, be weighed on a case-by-case basis, and include a plan for reintegration. Reentry talking circles are nonpunitive ways for rebuilding relationships and providing support. Replacing out-of-school suspensions with in-school suspensions can be a better option, as long as the in-school suspension room provides opportunities for rje processes.

What if the in-school suspension room was reframed as a student support room where

- trained circle facilitators (peers and/or adults) could assist students working through conflict, while at the same time teaching them about problem-solving skills?
- counselors could work with students to develop greater social and emotional capacities?
- academic support is provided, recognizing the link between academic failure and behavior?
- circle processes provide opportunities for students and staff to express frustrations and harms in ways that lead to healing of relationships?

In addition, consider replacing the school's student conduct code with some type of community agreement in which all members of the community—administrators, students, teachers, and staff—agree to a shared set of expectations about how to be together.

Rather than adults holding students accountable for things they themselves are not living into, a community agreement sends a message that adults and students alike are expected to live by restorative values.

Prepare Facilitators to Address Serious Harm

Facilitating circle processes when serious harm is involved requires preparation and experience. Facilitators need to be well trained in working with conflict, harm, and trauma. Facilitating circle processes or conferences in these situations is not as simple as putting people in a room together and having them talk it out. Without knowing how to facilitate, including adequately preparing participants in advance, there is a risk of revictimization and of creating more harm.

In our work with schools implementing rje practices, we have heard too many stories of educators attempting to facilitate circle processes after only a few hours of training. In one situation, a teacher brought together two boys who had been in a fight. Not understanding the context and failing to do any type of pre-conferencing, one boy began bullying the other boy in the circle process, causing further harm and casting doubt on the potential of rje to resolve conflicts. In another situation, a student, believing the circle was a safe place, began to open up emotionally about something personal. An unprepared facilitator, uncomfortable with the emotional response, exerted *power over* the student by interrupting the sharing and making suggestions. The facilitator's response violated the safe place and embarrassed the student in front of peers. Thus, we recommend that

111

schools have several highly trained people (teachers, administrators, or community members) on hand with enough experience to facilitate circles for incidents of serious harm.

Summary

Repairing harm and transforming conflict are important components of rje. When we prioritize healthy relationships and the dignity of each person, we are on the way to establishing restorative school cultures.

SECTION 3
Sustainable Growth

Restorative justice in education has incredible potential for anchoring society in beliefs and values that support well-being for all members of the learning community. As we conclude this Little Book, we leave you with a variety of suggestions and resources to help you nurture strong foundational root systems and healthy growth. Chapter 7 provides a list of suggestions for beginning sustainable rje work. The two appendixes provide resources and references that will assist you as you seek to learn more. These final insights, gleaned from years of work across North America, collaboration with educators, and an emerging research base, are still only a beginning. We are excited to see the growth that will continue to take place as the field of rje continues to evolve.

Chapter 7
A Tale of Two Schools: Sustainable Implementation

This chapter begins with two case studies of schools that have implemented rje, one of which could be seen as successful, the other unsuccessful. As you read the descriptions of the two schools, list the differences you see between their approaches to implementing rje. The chapter concludes with recommendations for implementation that have demonstrated greater effectiveness and sustainability.

Eastpoint Community School developed a five-year plan to integrate rje into its school culture. It included ongoing professional development; student leadership; and a focus on developing skills, in-depth knowledge, and a restorative ethos. At the end of the five years, new student and staff support systems had been implemented:

- Students, teachers, administrators, families, and communities were experiencing improved relationships at school.
- Rje policies had been developed.
- Suspension rates were down by 45 percent.
- Graduation rates had improved by 30 percent.
- The district asked representatives from Eastpoint to begin working with other schools to lead district-wide implementation.

Sprucedale Community School also developed a five-year plan. It included an initial training for all employees, with additional trainings for new employees each year. Rje practices were written into the student discipline code, and teachers were encouraged to include circle processes to build community in their classes. By the fifth year, the following had occurred:

- Most teachers had quit using circle processes, claiming that they were taking up too much time and were not effective for building community.
- Suspension rates were down, but teachers expressed frustration because nothing ever happened to students who were sent to the office.
- There was a general consensus among the students, teachers, administrators, families, and communities that rje at Sprucedale was not working.

What were the differences between the two schools? Many factors played into the two very different outcomes. The key difference between Eastpoint and Sprucedale was the depth of understanding of rje. We see this in how Eastpoint

- viewed rje as a holistic approach to school culture rather than just a discipline system.
- integrated theory and practice, and did not simply focus on skills development.
- infused rje into already existing systems rather than as a separate, tacked-on program.
- had ongoing, rather than one-time, professional development.

As we have worked with and learned from schools across North America, we have been able to see rje succeed and fail. Based on our research, practice, interactions, and conversations with educators, we have observed schools where changes occurred but where the approach fell apart when one particular rje advocate retired. We have seen places where the entire school system was trained in restorative justice practices, but when continued professional development and support were not available, teachers became discouraged and quit engaging with the practices.

A recent policy brief, authored by Gregory and Evans, identified five mis-implementation models—five ways in which rje has been implemented in unsustainable ways:[1] (1) Mandated top-down models that fail at collaborative decision-making, ignoring participants' readiness and/or resistance for innovation; (2) Narrowly defined models that hyperfocus on student behavior rather than holistic and comprehensive approaches to shifting school culture; (3)

Color-blind and power-blind models that ignore issues of power, justice, and equity; (4) Train and hope models that provide initial professional development with minimal "follow-up, coaching, demonstration, or performance feedback"(p. 14); and (5) Under-resourced and underfunded models that underestimate the time and support necessary for effective implementation.

When rje implementation fails, it does more than disrupt the rje initiative; it can leave students, educators, and families feeling frustrated, burned out, hopeless, and angry. For example, poorly equipped school administrators who begin with a train and hope model can implement rje practices that disempower educators by failing to address challenging behavior. While administrators are attempting to reduce suspensions, teachers can feel unsupported, discouraged, and prone to burnout. As another example, classroom teachers who engage with a color-blind and power-blind model may attribute student behavior to defiance and disrespect and miss the violation of dignity that students may be experiencing through curricular or pedagogical practices that perpetuate microaggressions, marginalization, or oppression.

If our work as restorative justice educators is to be sustainable, we have to build programs that lay strong foundations and provide wide, deep root systems. Extending the analogy of the plant with which we began, the tree depicted earlier in this book is able to grace the landscape because it has robust root systems that are at least as large as the crown above the ground.

It is our hope that rje continues to move from the margins to the mainstreams of education, gracing the landscape. For this to be accomplished, we offer the following recommendations for increasing the sustainability of rje:

- *Remember the seeds and the roots.* Consistently engage with the core beliefs and values through activities and action. Take time to creatively explore how to nurture a relational culture that permeates all aspects of the school climate. Nurture the root system at every stage of development.[2]
- *Start slowly and confidently.* Invite people to engage as they are ready. People support change at different rates when they feel honored and respected and when they realize that the core beliefs and values resonate with their own. Respect and listen to those reticent to buy in; sometimes they see things we cannot—and it is the restorative way to hold with dignity all members of the community. Though whole-school implementation is ideal, this will occur only when individuals see the connection to themselves. Start with members of the school community who are ready and grow from there. Resist models for implementing change that are hierarchical and often do not model relational, restorative beliefs and values.
- *Model continually and consistently.* As you support rje implementation, model the ethos, values, and principles in all you do. If you hope for students to treat one another with respect and dignity, the adults must treat one another this way. Begin implementing the core principles and practices of rje with the adults in the school community. Ensure circle processes are used in staff and other adult meetings. Experiencing circles as adults will

119

help implement an authentic relational ethos with students. As adults engage, then introduce it to the students.

- *Provide ongoing professional development opportunities that focus on both underlying beliefs and values as well as principles for practices and specific skills.* Recognize that the term "training" can denote a skills-based experience and lead educators to conclude that rje is a strategy for their "classroom management toolbox." Though skills are necessary, "educating" about the rje ethos is required for transformational change. Sometimes this professional development can be provided internally by colleagues, students, or caregivers who are engaging with rje. At other times, external expertise will propel implementation forward.

- *Don't do it alone.* If you are the rje champion in your context, organize an rje implementation team as soon as possible. Consider teachers, parents, caregivers, students, staff, and community members who are curious or committed to exploring with you. Be sure there are both "insiders," people who know the context of the school well, and "outsiders," those who may be able to see the context from a different angle.

- *Remember the power of youth leadership.* Engage children and youth as soon as possible. When they are given opportunities and support to take on leadership roles, they have the potential to deeply strengthen the culture of the school.[3]

- *Consider representation on your implementation team, working to ensure that those with various identities have a seat at the table when decisions are*

120

being made. Diversity of opinions, experiences, and perspectives can strengthen efforts to transform school culture and enact policies and practices that support all members of the learning community.

- *Be strategic.* As a team, begin by taking six to twelve months to become knowledgeable about restorative justice. Study, read, and participate in professional development. Visit other places where rje is working well and learn from those schools. Make a careful plan that is specific to your context. Don't forget to examine the current vision and mission of the school as these often already use the language of well-being. Demonstrate how rje can support what already exists.

- *Create a long-term plan* that takes into account the need for mindsets to shift, policies to change, and educational opportunities for all members of the community to be provided. This takes time and requires a long-range vision, along with concrete implementation steps. Rather than solely focusing on outcomes, focus on adherence to the principles and values, realizing that small steps in the right direction are more impactful than huge initiatives that are not grounded.

- *Develop an evaluation process* that guides your implementation from the beginning. As you grow, use that evaluation process to monitor and evaluate your plan to ensure that you are staying on track. As part of that evaluation plan, be sure to examine current policies for places that may be undermining rje (e.g., most student codes of conduct include lists of behavioral consequences that disregard restoration).[4]

121

- *Start with the assets you have.* What is already happening at your school that reflects rje beliefs and values? Celebrate these assets and then expand. For example, if your school is already adding trauma-informed practices, consider connecting the rje initiative to what is already in place. If it is actively engaged in anti-racism and cultural diversity, make the connection to rje explicit. Also, identify what is happening that contradicts rje. How can you use your assets to make changes? Remember that rje implementation should impact all aspects of the school, including family and community engagement and discipline practices, as well as pedagogical practices, curriculum content, architectural/physical design, etc.
- *Make use of any financial resources to appoint full-time rje coordinators* who can provide internal professional development and facilitate circles for serious harm and conflict. However, where funds are not available, reconfigure current roles so that existing staff can provide consistency and leadership. Funding should not determine the degree to which you hold tightly to the values and principles of rje; it is not about adding a program, but about gradually changing what already exists. It will be beneficial if people in specific roles in the school (e.g., curriculum programs, student life, guidance, discipline, etc.) are included early so they can initiate whole-school change. Regardless of the availability of resources, the plan must always include creating a strong foundational team that will remain intact over time and when change

occurs (e.g., when supportive administrators or lead teachers leave).

Restorative justice in education is not a program; it's a framework. Returning again to Lorraine Stutzman Amstutz and Judy Mullet's book, *The Little Book of Restorative Discipline for Schools*:

"We don't propose a cookie-cutter approach to restorative [justice]; to imply such would oversimplify complex and diverse community situation. Rather, a restorative approach is a philosophy or framework that can guide us as we design programs and make decisions within our particular settings."

What develops in your context will be unique. What it will share with others who are implementing a restorative justice culture is a root system—the common belief and understanding of humanity as being worthy and interconnected. What we provide in this Little Book is a careful exploration of those roots so you can strengthen the growth of rje where you are.

Summary

In summary, restorative justice in education is a comprehensive and holistic approach to education. The types of change that we believe rje can bring about are not limited to reductions in suspension rates, improved student behavior, or even improved academic achievement, although those outcomes are certainly included. What we hope for is the transformation of school cultures such that all members of the learning community—including students, teachers, staff, administrators, parents, and caregivers—feel that they belong. We long for schools where students and teachers are engaged in active and enthusiastic learning and where everyone—regardless of their race, gender, sexual orientation, ethnicity, religion, language, ability, or class—is valued and provided with what they need to grow and learn. Cultural transformation is possible when rje is implemented in a context where people are honored as worthy and interconnected.

Resources

The following resources are recommended for implementing sustainable rje. This list is not exhaustive, but will provide resources for getting started.

Books

Aquino, E., H. B. Manchester & A. Wadhwa. (2021). *The Little Book of Youth Engagement in Restorative Justice: Intergenerational Partnerships for Just and Equitable Schools.* Good Books.

Bianci, H. (1994). *Justice as Sanctuary: Toward a New System of Crime Control.* Wipf and Stock.

Boyes-Watson, C., & K. Pranis. (2020). *Circle Forward.* St. Paul, MN: Living Justice Press.

———. (2010). *Heart of Hope.* St. Paul, MN: Living Justice Press.

Brown, M. (2018). *Creating Restorative Schools: Setting Schools up to Succeed.* Living Justice Press.

Brummer, J. (2021). *Building a Trauma-Informed Restorative School: Skills and Approaches for Improving Culture and Behavior.* Jessica Kingsley Publishers.

Burnett, N., & Thorsborne, M. (2015). *Restorative Practice and Special Needs: A Practical Guide to*

Working Restoratively with Young People. Jessica Kingsley Publishers.

Claassen, R., & R. Claassen. (2008). *Discipline that Restores.* South Carolina: BookSurge Publishing.

———. (2015). *Making Things Right: Activities that Teach Restorative Justice, Conflict Resolution, Mediation, and Discipline that Restores.* North Charleston, SC: BookSurge Publishing.

Davis, F. E. (2019). *The Little Book of Race and Restorative Justice: Black Lives, Healing, and US Social Transformation.* Good Books.

Graveline, F. J. (1998). *Circle Works: Transforming Eurocentric Consciousness.* Fernwood Publishing.

Hendry, R. (2009). *Building and Restoring Respectful Relationships in Schools: A Guide to Using Restorative Practice.* Abingdon, UK: Routledge.

Holtham, J. (2009). *Taking Restorative Justice to Schools: A Doorway to Discipline.* Del Hayes Press.

Hopkins, B. (2004). *Just Schools: A Whole School Approach to Restorative Justice.* London: Jessica Kingsley Publishers.

———. (2011). *The Restorative Classroom: Using Restorative Approaches to Foster Effective Learning.* London: Optimus Education.

Hopkins, B. (ed.) 2016. *Restorative Theory in Practice: Insights into What Works and Why.* Jessica Kingsley Press.

Karp, D. (2013). *The Little Book of Restorative Justice for Colleges and Universities.* Intercourse, PA: Good Books.

Kelly, V., & Thorsborne, M., eds. (2014). *The Psychology of Emotion in Restorative Practice: How Affect Script*

Psychology Explains How and Why Restorative Practice Works. Jessica Kingsley Publishers.

Lewis., T., & C. Stauffer. (eds). (2021). *Listening to the Movement: Essays on New Growth and New Challenges in Restorative Justice.* Cascade Books.

Morrison, B. (2007). *Restoring Safe School Communities: A Whole School Response to Bullying, Violence and Alienation.* Sydney, Australia: The Federation Press.

Pointer, L., K. McGooey & H. Farrar. (2020). *The Little Book of Restorative Teaching Tools: Games, Activities, and Simulations for Understanding Restorative Justice Practices.* Good Books.

Pranis, K. (2005). *The Little Book of Circle Processes: A New/Old Approach to Peacemaking.* Intercourse, PA: Good Books.

Pranis, K., B. Stuart & M. Wedge. (2003). *Peacemaking Circles: From Crime to Community.* St. Paul, MN: Living Justice Press.

Reimer, K. E. (2019). *Adult Intentions, Student Perceptions: How Restorative Justice Is Used in Schools to Control and to Engage.* Information Age Publishing.

Riestenberg, N. (2012). *Circle in the Square: Building Community and Repairing Harm in School.* St. Paul, MN: Living Justice Press.

Sellman, E., H. Cremin & G. McCluskey. (2013). *Restorative Approaches to Conflict in Schools: Interdisciplinary Perspectives on Whole-school Approaches to Managing Relationships.* Abingdon, UK: Routledge.

Stutzman Amstutz, L., & J. H. Mullet. (2005). *The Little Book of Restorative Discipline for Schools.* Intercourse, PA: Good Books.

127

Thorsborne, M., & P. Blood. (2013). *Implementing Restorative Practice in Schools: A Practical Guide to Transforming School Communities.* London: Jessica Kingsley Publishers.

Thorsborne, M., Riestenberg, N., & McCluskey, G. (2019). *Getting More out of Restorative Practice in Schools: Practical Approaches to Improve School Wellbeing and Strengthen Community Engagement.* Jessica Kingsley Publishers.

Valandra, E. C., & Hoksila, W. W. (2020). *Colorizing Restorative Justice: Voicing Our Realities.* Living Justice Press.

Wadhwa, A. (2015). *Restorative Justice in Urban Schools: Disrupting the School-to-Prison Pipeline.* London, Routledge Press.

Winn, M. T. (2018). *Justice on Both Sides: Transforming Education through Restorative Justice.* Harvard Education Press.

Winn, M. T., H. Graham & R. R. Alfred. (2019). *Restorative Justice in the English Language Arts Classroom.* National Council of Teachers of English.

Winn, M. T., & L. T. Winn (eds.). (2021). *Restorative Justice in Education: Transforming Teaching and Learning Through the Disciplines.* Harvard Education Press.

Yoder, C. (2007). *The Little Book of Trauma Healing.* Intercourse, PA: Good Books.

Zehr, H. (1990). *Changing Lenses: A New Focus for Crime and Justice.* Scottdale, PA: Herald Press.

———. (2002). *The Little Book of Restorative Justice.* Intercourse, PA: Good Books.

———. (2002). *Journey to belonging,* in *Restorative Justice: Theoretical Foundations,* eds. E. G. M

Weitekamp and H. J. Kerner, 23–25. Cullompton, UK: Willan Publishing.

Organizations and Websites

Adverse Childhood Experiences: http://www.cdc.gov/violenceprevention/acestudy/index.html

Bowen, Skye (2021). Restorative Justice: It's Complicated. https://www.youtube.com/watch?v=-X_EmYjLHE8

Canadian Restorative Justice Consortium: https://www.crjc.ca

Center for Restorative Justice (Suffolk University): http://www.suffolk.edu/college/centers/14521.php

Center for Restorative Process: http://www.centerforrestorativeprocess.com

Circle Formations: https://youtu.be/ulAgpSRHouo

Colorado Restorative Justice: http://www.rjcolorado.org

Community Justice Initiatives: Educating for Peacebuilding: http://www.cjibc.org/peacebuilding_program

Community Justice for Youth Institute (Chicago): http://cjyiorg.publishpath.com/cjyi-services

Connect RP (Ireland): https://www.connectrp.ie

Discipline That Restores (Fresno Pacific University): http://disciplinethatrestores.org

Eastern Mennonite University Restorative Justice in Education Resources: https://emu.edu/maed/resources

Institute for Restorative Justice and Restorative Dialogue (University of Texas): http://www.utexas.edu/research/cswr/rji/index.html

LBRJE Book Club: https://www.relationshipsfirstnl.com/rfpodcast

Minnesota Department of Education Restorative Practices: http://www.education.state.mn.us/MDE/SchSup/SchSafety/RestorativePractices/index.html

National Association for Community and Restorative Justice: http://www.nacrj.org

National Centre for Collaboration in Indigenous Education: https://www.nccie.ca/lessonplan/the-circle/

Project on Restorative Justice (Skidmore College): http://www.skidmore.edu/campusrj/

Relationships First: Restorative Justice Education in NL: www.relationshipsfirstnl.com/

A Restorative Approach: John Martin Junior High (Halifax): https://www.youtube.com/watch?v=ggRTMNZVHYw&feature=youtu.be

Restorative Circles: http://www.restorativecircles.org

Restorative Justice Institute of Maine: http://www.rjimaine.org

Restorative Justice International (Fresno Pacific University):http://www.restorativejusticeinternational.com

Restorative Justice Music Education: https://www.restorativejusticemusiceducation.com

Restorative Justice for Oakland Youth (RJOY): http://rjoyoakland.org

Restorative Justice Project of the Midcoast: http://www.rjpmidcoast.org

Restorative Lab: https://restorativelab.ca

Restorative Schools Australia: https://restorativeschoolsaustralia.org/

The Restorative Way: https://www.restorativeway.com

Ripples of Relationship: https://youtu.be/NYVidRSxCyE

St. Croix Valley Restorative Justice: http://www.
scvrjp.org

Two-Eared Listening for Deeper Understanding:
www.twoearedlistening.com

Zehr Institute of Restorative Justice (Eastern
Mennonite University): https://zehr-institute.org/

Professional Development and/or Education

Many of the websites listed in the preceding
section offer professional development videos and
information. In addition, these opportunities exist for
more formal education:

The Center for Justice and Peacebuilding at Eastern
Mennonite University offers a master's degree
and an 18-hour certificate in restorative justice.
It also regularly offers webinars, workshops,
and summer courses: http://www.emu.edu/cjp/
restorative-justice/%20/

Eastern Mennonite University Master's of Education
Department offers a concentration in restorative
justice in education, as well as a 15-hour graduate
certificate in restorative justice in education: http://
www.emu.edu/maed/

Simon Fraser University offers two certificate programs in restorative justice, one foundational and
one with an education focus: https://www.sfu.ca/
continuing-studies/courses/crj/restorative-justice
-in-educational-settings.html

Suffolk University Center for Restorative Justice
offers professional development and a professional
certificate in restorative justice for "practitioners

in the fields of education, law, criminal/juvenile justice, social work and community-based conflict resolution": https://www.suffolk.edu/cas/centers-institutes/center-for-restorative-justice

Endnotes

Preface

1. Use of the lowercase "rje" is an intentional choice to emphasize that restorative justice education is not the name of a particular program or approach, but rather an overall way of being that encompasses a deep understanding of the role of relationships in the context of teaching and learning.

2. Fronius, T., S. Darling-Hammond, H. Persson, H., S. Guckenburg, S., N. Hurley & A. Petrosino. 2019. *Restorative Justice in U.S. Schools: An Updated Research Review*. WestEd.

    Gregory, A., & K. Evans. 2020. *The Starts and Stumbles of Restorative Justice in Education: Where do we go from here?* National Education Policy Center.

    Reimer, K. (2019). *Adult Intentions, Student Perceptions: How Restorative Justice is Used in Schools to Control and to Engage*. IAP Publishing.

    Skiba, R. J., M. I. Arredondo & M. K. Rausch. 2014. *New and developing research on disparities in discipline. Discipline Disparities Series*. The Equity Project at Indiana University.

    Morgan, E., N. Saloman, M. Plotkin & R. Cohen. 2014. *School Discipline Consensus Report*. Council of State Governments Justice Center.

    Gonzalez, T., H. Sattler & A. J. Buth. 2018. *New directions in whole-school restorative justice implementation. Conflict Resolution Quarterly*, 36: 207–220.

    Gonzalez, T., & R. Epstein. 2021. *Building Foundations of Health and Wellbeing in Schools: A Study of Restorative Practices and Girls of Color. Georgetown Law Center on Poverty and Inequality*.

3. Vaandering, D. 2011. A faithful compass: Rethinking the term restorative justice to find clarity. *Contemporary Justice Review 14*(3):307–28.
4. See Acknowledgements and Resource sections for details.
5. See Acknowledgements and Resource sections for details.
6. Lilla Watson attributes this quote to an Aboriginal Rights group in Queensland she worked with in the early 1970's.

Acknowledgments

1. Bowen, Skye. 2021. Restorative Justice: It's Complicated. https://www.youtube.com/watch?v=-X_EmYjLHE8

   Bowen, Skye. 2021. Push Out: Anti-racist Reads. https://www.listennotes.com/podcasts/anti-racist/ep-03-pushout-ft-skye-bowen-2-DYNJVmQ4z/

   Bowen, Skye. 2021. Building to Last with Educator, Champion and Advocate Skye Bowen. Episode 20 of Building to Last: https://voiced.ca/podcast_episode_post/building-to-last-with-educator-champion-and-advocate-skye-bowen/
2. Davis, F. 2019. *The Little Book of Race and Restorative Justice*. Good Books.
3. Valandra, E. 2020. *Colorizing Restorative Justice*. Living Justice Press.
4. Aquino, E., H. Manchester & A. Wadhwa. 2021. *The Little Book of Youth Engagement in Restorative Justice*. Good Books.
5. Winn, M. 2018. *Justice on Both Sides*. Harvard Education Press.

   Winn, M., H. Graham & R. Renjitham. 2020. *Restorative Justice in the English Language Arts Classroom*. NCTE.

   Winn, M., & T. Winn. 2021. *Restorative Justice in Education: Transforming Teaching and Learning Through the Disciplines*. Harvard Education Press.

Chapter 1

1. This holistic definition of justice draws on ancient and contemporary Indigenous and spiritual traditions— in particular, the broad understanding of circle connectedness and justice as the "good way" and the Judeo-Christian concepts of shalom and covenant. See Chapter 4 for more information.

   Bianchi, H. 1994. *Justice as Sanctuary*. Indiana University Press.

   Hadley, M. 2001. *The Spiritual Roots of Restorative Justice*. SUNY Press.

   McCaslin, W. 2005. *Justice as Healing: Indigenous Ways: Writings on Community Peacemaking and Restorative Justice from the Native Law Centre*. Living Justice Press.

   Pranis, K., B. Stuart & M. Wedge. 2003. *Peacemaking Circles: From Crime to Community*. Living Justice Press.

   Ross, R. 1996. *Returning to the Teachings*. Penguin.

   Wolterstorff, N. 2008. *Justice: Rights and Wrongs*. Princeton University Press.

   Zehr, H. 2005. *Changing Lenses: A New Focus for Crime and Justice,* 3rd ed. Herald Press.

2. Pranis, K. 2005. *The Little Book of Circle Processes: A New/Old Approach to Peacemaking,* 24. Good Books.

   All of the books relating to restorative justice in the Little Book Series identify in various ways this philosophical foundation for restorative justice. This Little Book seeks to highlight the importance of this philosophy.

3. Educational reform movements, particularly in the United States, place a great deal of pressure on schools to improve test scores, often with serious consequences for failing to do so. Curricular decisions are often made with testing in mind, rather than the needs or well-being of students, creating a narrow curriculum that is primarily test-driven. This excessive use of testing as a way to measure and rank both students and teachers, as well as schools and districts, distracts from relational

135

pedagogy espoused by restorative justice. For more about testing, see: Ken Robinson. 2010. "Changing education paradigms." https://www.youtube.com/watch?v = 2svFFaEShpM

4. Morrison, B. 2010. From social control to social engagement: Enabling the "time and space" to talk through restorative justice and responsive regulation, in *Contemporary Issues in Criminology Theory and Research*, Eds. R. Rosenfeld, K. Quinet, and C. Garcia (pp. 97–106). Wadsworth Cengage Learning.

Chapter 2

1. Chief Mi'sel Joe. 2021. Two-Eared Listening for Deeper Understanding: Restorative Justice in Newfoundland and Labrador. www.twoearedlistening.com

2. Bowen, S. 2021. Restorative Justice Education: Returning to Our Roots.

3. For specific examples of this invitation, see: F. Davis. 2019. *The Little Book of Race and Restorative Justice*. Good Books.

   Valandra, E. 2020. Undoing the first harm: Settlers in restorative justice. In *Colorizing Restorative Justice: Voicing Our Realities*. Living Justice Press. Chapter 18.

   Breton, D. 2005. Digging deeper: Challenges for restorative justice. In *Justice as Healing*. Living Justice Press, pp. 409–34.

4. See Acknowledgments and Resource sections.

5. *Disproportionality* refers to the overrepresentation of some groups of students within school discipline systems, leading to higher suspension and expulsion rates and contributing to what has been termed "the school-to-prison pipeline," a phenomenon that shows that students with higher suspension rates are more likely to end up incarcerated.

6. Gregory, A., R. J. Skiba & K. Mediratta. 2017. Eliminating disparities in school discipline: A framework for intervention. *Review of Research in Education, 41*(1), 253-278. https://doi.org/10.3102/0091732x17690499

Gregory, A., & K. Clawson. 2016. The potential of restorative approaches to discipline for narrowing racial and gender disparities. In R. J. Skiba, K. Mediratta & M. K. Rausch (eds.), *Inequality in school discipline: Research and practice to reduce disparities* (pp. 153–170). Palgrave Macmillan.

7. National Centre for Truth and Reconciliation. 2015. *Truth and Reconciliation Calls To Action.*

8. Truth and Reconciliation Commission of Canada. 2015. *Canada's Residential Schools: Missing Children and Unmarked Burials.* McGill-Queen's University Press.

9. Sinclair, M. 2015. National Centre for Truth and Reconciliation. https://www.youtube.com/watch?v=wjx2zDvyzsU

10. Flood, D. 2012. *Healing the Gospel: A Radical Vision for Grace, Justice, and the Cross.* Cascade Books.

Mennonite Central Committee 2016. *The Doctrine of Discovery.* https://www.youtube.com/watch?v=WLh 4INBdvOk

Assembly of First Nations (January 2019). *Dismantling the Doctrine of Discovery.* Ottawa.

Zehr, H. 2015. Covenant justice: The Biblical alternative. In *Changing Lenses.* MennoMedia. Chapter 8.

11. As authors, this is our story. As non-Indigenous people, we have been influenced by the varied faith-traditions we have grown up in and been a part of. For both of us, we have been troubled by the hypocrisy present in teachings, traditions, and practices of our particular faith communities. For both of us, restorative justice and rje have created opportunities for us to critique, reevaluate, and call our faith communities to do better. Through all of this, restorative justice has led us to rediscovering the essence of our faith, a faith that was never intended to be interpreted through the lenses of colonization and oppressive power.

12. Winn, M. 2018. *Justice on Both Sides.* Harvard Education Press. See also, https://diversity.ucdavis.edu/sites/g/files/dgvnsk731/files/inline-files/Winn_TeachingWorks_5PS.pdf

13. For information about the history of VORP and VOC, see: Sullivan, D., & L. Tifft. 2006. *Handbook of restorative justice: A global perspective.* Milton Park, UK: Routledge.
14. Skiba, R. J. 2000. *Zero tolerance, zero evidence: An analysis of school disciplinary practice.* Indiana Education Policy Center.
15. Anderson, C. L. 2004. Double jeopardy: The modern dilemma for juvenile justice. *University of Pennsylvania Law Review* 152(3): 1181–1219.
16. CBC. April 13, 2007. Ontario agrees to end zero-tolerance school policy. http://www.cbc.ca/news/canada/toronto/ontario-agrees-to-end-zero-tolerance-school-policy-1.671464.
17. American Psychological Association. (2008). Are zero tolerance policies effective in the schools? An evidentiary review and recommendations. *American Psychologist* 63(9): 852–62.
18. U.S. Department of Education, Office for Civil Rights. October 26, 2010. Dear colleague letter: Harassment and bullying. http:// www2.ed.gov/about/offices/list/ocr/letters/colleague-201010.html.
19. Morrison, B., & D. Vaadering. 2012. Restorative justice: Pedagogy, praxis, and discipline. *Journal of School Violence,* 11(2).
20. See Teaching Works working papers such as: https://diversity.ucdavis.edu/sites/g/files/dgvnsk731/files/inline-files/Winn_TeachingWorks_5PS.pdf
21. https://emu.edu/maed/restorative-justice
22. https://www.sfu.ca/continuing-studies/courses/crj/restorative-justice-in-educational-settings.html
23. Gregory, A., & K. Evans. 2020. *The Starts and Stumbles of Restorative Justice in Education: Where do we go from here?* National Education Policy Center.
24. Several key documents to guide in-depth engagement with anti-racist and culturally informed practice include:
    Evans, K., B. Morrison & D. Vaandering. 2019. Critical Race Theory and Restorative Justice Education in

Listening to the Movement: Essays on new growth and new challenges in Restorative Justice, Wipf & Stock Publishers.

Boyes-Watson, C., & K. Pranis. 2020. Module 14: Moving Toward Racial Equity—Starting with the Adults. In *Circle Forward*. Living Justice Press.

Joseph, A., R. Hnilica & M. Hansen. 2021. Using Restorative Practices to Reduce Racially Disproportionate School Suspensions: The Barriers School Leaders Should Consider During the First Year of Implementation. *Taboo: The Journal of Culture and Education, 20(2)*.

Lustick, H. 2020. Culturally Responsive Restorative Discipline. *Educational Studies. 56(6). pp. 555-583.*

Parker, C. 2020. Who's in and who's out? Problematizing peacemaking circles in diverse classrooms. In *Colorizing Restorative Justice*. Living Justice Press, pp. 65–86.

Song, S., J. Eddy, H. Thompson, B. Adams & J. Beskow. 2020. Restorative consultation in schools: A systematic review and call for restorative justice science to promote anti- racism and social justice. Journal Of Educational And Psychological Consultation, 30(4).

Wadhwa, A. 2020. "What do you want, reparations?" Racial Microaggressions and restorative justice. In *Colorizing Restorative Justice*. Living Justice Press, pp. 159–172.

Wilson, Sheryl. 2020. Calling out whiteness. In *Colorizing Restorative Justice*. Living Justice Press, pp. 103–114.

25. Brummer, J. 2020. *Building a Trauma-Informed Restorative School*. Jessica Kingsley Publishers.

Chapter 3

1. Zehr, H. 1990. *Changing Lenses: A New Focus for Crime and Justice*. Herald Press.
2. Pajares, M. F. 1992. Teachers' beliefs and educational research: Cleaning up a messy construct. *Review of Educational Research* 62(3): 307-32.

Willard, D. 1999. *Spiritual formation meets the gospel.* Regent College Lectures.

3. This discussion regarding Western neoliberalism and rj is articulated well in:

Llewellyn, K., & J. Llewellyn. 2015. A restorative approach to learning: Relational theory as feminist pedagogy in universities, in *Feminist Pedagogy in Higher Education: Critical Theory and Practice*, Eds. T. Light, J. Nicholas & R. Bondy, 11–32. Wilfrid Laurier University Press.

4. Boyes-Watson, C., & K. Pranis. 2020. *Circle Forward.* Living Justice Press.

5. These three values essential for relationship are identified in: Llewellyn, J. 2012. Restorative justice: Thinking relationally about justice, in *Being Relational,* Eds. J. Downie & J. Llewellyn. Vancouver: UBC Press.

6. For more details, see:

Vaandering, D. 2011. A faithful compass: Rethinking the term restorative justice to find clarity. *Contemporary Justice Review* 14(3): 307–28.

Other questions could be asked to critically self-reflect, such as, "Am I focused on needs or punishment? Am I seeing this person as relational or independent? Am I respecting this person as unconditionally worthy? Am I creating conditions for this person's worth? The three questions chosen for this Little Book are suggested as a way to consistently expose how personal core beliefs align with the core beliefs of rje. They also keep the focus on personal responsibility and do not allow for deflecting responsibility to others.

7. Morrison, B., & D. Vaandering 2012. Restorative justice: Pedagogy, praxis, and discipline. *Journal of School Violence* 11(2): 138–55.

Chapter 4

1. For an in-depth discussion of the concepts of shalom and *sedeqah*, see:

Marshall, C. 2005. *Little Book of Biblical Justice.* Intercourse, PA: Good Books.

2. Akrami, Amir. 2016. Yale Divinity School, personal correspondence.

3. Yazzie, R. "Life comes from it": Navajo justice concepts. https://www.amizade.org/wp-content/uploads/2011/07/LifeComesFromIt.doc.

4. Elliot, E. 2011. The geometry of individuals and relationships, in *Security with care,* 139. Blackpoint, NS: Fernwood Publishers.

5. Franklin, U., & M. Swenarchuk. 2006. *The Ursula Franklin reader.* Toronto: Between the Lines.

6. Boyes-Watson, C., & K. Pranis. 2015. *Circle forward,* 139. St. Paul, MN: Living Justice Press.

7. American Psychological Association. 2008. Are zero tolerance policies effective in the schools? An evidentiary review and recommendations. *American Psychologist* 63(9): 852–62.
   Although we focused on the student in this example, it is important to consider the harm experienced by educators who are repeatedly expected to comply with policies, such as zero tolerance, that violate their own conscience.

8. Forty years of data demonstrate this disproportionality. See for example:
   Fenning, P., & J. Rose. 2007. Overrepresentation of African American students in exclusionary discipline: The role of school policy. *Urban Education* 42(6): 536–59.
   Gregory, A., R. J. Skiba & P. A. Noguera. 2010. The achievement gap and the discipline gap: Two sides of the same coin? *Educational Researcher* 39(1): 59–68.
   U.S. Department of Education, Office for Civil Rights. October 26, 2010. Dear colleague letter: Harassment and bullying. http:// www2.ed.gov/about/offices/list/ocr/letters/colleague-201010.html.

9. Standard VI reads: "Candidates demonstrate knowledge of how theories and research about social justice, diversity, equity, student identities, and schools as institutions can enhance students' opportunities to learn in English Language Arts." Located at www.ncte.org.

10. Sullivan, D., and L. Tifft. 2001. *Restorative justice: Healing the foundations of our everyday lives*, 167. Monsey, NY: Willow Tree Press.

11. For more information about addressing students' needs in schools, see:

    Deci, E. L., & R. M. Ryan. 1991. A motivational approach to self: Integration in personality. *Perspectives on motivation*. Lincoln, NE: University of Nebraska Press.

    Glasser, W. 1985. Discipline has never been the problem and isn't the problem now. *Theory into Practice* 24(4): 241–46.

12. Zehr, H. 2002. Journey to belonging, in *Restorative justice: Theoretical foundations*, Eds. E. G. M. Weitekamp and H. J. Kerner, 23–25. Cullompton, UK: Willan Publishing.

13. Freire, P. 1970. *Pedagogy of the oppressed*. New York: Continuum Press.

14. Vygotsky, L. S. 1986. *Thought and language*, 39. Cambridge, MA: MIT Press.

15. See more about differentiation in:

    Tomlinson, C. A. 2014. *The differentiated classroom: Responding to the needs of all learners*. Alexandria, VA: ASCD.

16. For more information, see:

    Ladson-Billings, G. 1990. Culturally relevant teaching: Effective instruction for black students. *The College Board Review* 7(15): 20–25.

    Ladson-Billings, G. 1995. Toward a theory of culturally relevant pedagogy. *American Educational Research Journal* 32(3): 465–91.

17. Whitewashing refers to the practice of looking at diversity through the lens of the majority, without considering the perspectives of those who daily experience discrimination. If we really want to avoid whitewashing, we need to create more spaces for marginalized youth to share their perspectives. More information about integrating equity into the curriculum can be found in:
Gorski, P., and Swalwell, K. 2015. Equity literacy for all. *Educational Leadership* 72(6): 34–40.

18. For example, see:
U.S. Department of Education, Office for Civil Rights. October 26, 2010. Dear colleague letter: Harassment and bullying. Retrieved from http:// www2.ed.gov/ about/offices/list/ocr/letters/colleague-201010.html.

19. The works of Paulo Freire and bell hooks create a framework for understanding rje more broadly, both in concepts here in this chapter and in our understanding of the humanization of one another. See also:
Vaandering, D. 2010. The significance of critical theory for restorative justice in education. *Review of Education, Pedagogy, and Cultural Studies* 32(2):145–76.

20. Vaandering, D. 2010. The significance of critical theory for restorative justice in education. *Review of Education, Pedagogy, and Cultural Studies* 32(2):145–76.
In this article, Vaandering talks extensively about the hidden curriculum that exists when teachers are unaware of their implicit biases.

21. For more information about rje and pedagogy, we suggest reading Maisha Winn's work on pedagogy: and Christina Parker's work on justice and equity within Circle processes:
Winn, M. T., H. Graham & R. R. Alfred. 2019. Restorative justice in the English language arts classroom. National Council of Teachers of English.
Winn, M. T., & L. T. Winn (eds.). 2021. Restorative justice in education: Transforming teaching and

learning through the disciplines. Harvard Education Press.

Parker, C., & K. Bickmore. 2020. Complexity in restorative justice education circles: Power and privilege in voicing perspectives about sexual health, identities, and relationships. *Journal of Moral Education.*

22. Ladson-Billings, G. 1995. Toward a theory of culturally relevant pedagogy. *American Educational Research Journal* 32(3): 465–91.

23. http://www.schooltalkdc.org/

24. https://specialedcoop.org/

25. See also the I'm Determined program sponsored by the Virginia Department of Education: www.imdetermined.org/

Chapter 5

1. Clinton, J. 2013. *The power of adult child relationships: Connection is the key.* Ontario: Queen's Printer for Ontario.

2. Boyes-Watson, C., and K. Pranis. 2015. *Circle forward,* 17–19. St. Paul, MN: Living Justice Press.
It provides a similar but more detailed explanation of power in the context of rje.

3. This matrix is a slight variation on several others. See for example:
Vaandering, D. 2013. A window on relationships: Reflecting critically on a current restorative justice theory. *Restorative Justice: An International Journal* 1(3): 311–33.

4. Elliot, E. 2011. The geometry of individuals and relationships, in *Security with care.* Blackpoint, NS: Fernwood Publishers.
This concept is the impetus behind using the reflective questions *Am I honoring, Am I measuring,* and *What message am I sending?* with all relationships identified in Figure 5.2. As each ripple is described, take a moment

to ask these questions to critically assess your relationships and open up possibilities for change.

5. Vaandering, D. 2014. Relational restorative justice pedagogy in educator professional development. *Curriculum Inquiry* 44:4.

   Also see descriptive video of this concept called Ripples of Relationship at: https://www.relationshipsfirstnl.com/videos

6. Figure 5.2 used with permission. See:

   Vaandering, D. 2014. Relational restorative justice pedagogy in educator professional development. *Curriculum Inquiry* 44(4): 508–30.

7. Nelson, M. 1999. Becoming Metis, in *At Home on the Earth: Becoming Native to Our Place*, 115. Berkeley, CA: University of California Press.

8. Boyes-Watson, C., and K. Pranis. 2015. *Circle forward*, 23. St. Paul, MN: Living Justice Press.

Chapter 6

1. Zehr, H. 1990. *Changing lenses: A new focus for crime and justice*, 199. Scottdale, PA: Herald Press.

2. Ibid.

3. Casella, R. 2003. Zero tolerance policy in schools: Rationale, consequences, and alternatives. *Teachers College Record* 105(5): 872-92.

4. American Psychological Association. 2008. Are zero tolerance policies effective in the schools? An evidentiary review and recommendations. *American Psychologist* 63(9): 852–62.

5. The ACEs study looks at ten questions related to childhood experiences that potentially have a negative impact on emotional health. A person with a high ACE score has had multiple Adverse Childhood Experiences. See more information on the ACE Study here: https://www.cdc.gov/violenceprevention/aces/index.html

6. Yoder, C. 2007. *The little book of trauma healing*. Intercourse, PA: Good Books.

7. Yehuda, R., N. P. Daskalakis, L. M. Bierer, et al. 2016. *Holocaust exposure induced intergenerational effects on FKBP5 methylation. Biological Psychiatry.* 80(5). p. 372–80.

   Limmena, M. 2021. *How intergeneratinal trauma affects Indigenous communities. Science Borealis.* https://blog.scienceborealis.ca/how-intergenerational-trauma-affects-indigenous-communities/

   Middelton-Moz, J., F. Mishna, R. Martell, C. Williams & S. Zuberi. 2021. *Indigenous trauma and resilience: pathways to 'bridging the river' in social work education, Social Work Education*

8. For more information about Walla Walla, consider hosting a viewing of the documentary *Paper Tigers.* More information can be found at https://www.wwcc.edu/blog/paper-tigers/.

9. Hicks, D. 2011. *Dignity: Its essential role in resolving conflict.* New Haven, CT: Yale University Press.

10. Zehr, H. 2002. *The little book of restorative justice,* 37. Intercourse, PA: Good Books.

11. Stutzman Amstutz, L., & J. H. Mullet. 2005. *The little book of restorative discipline for schools,* 15. Intercourse, PA: Good Books.

12. Sullivan, D., & L. Tifft. 2001. *Restorative justice: Healing the foundations of our everyday lives.* Monsey, NY: Willow Tree Press.

13. Dewey, J. 1922. Human nature and conduct: An introduction to social psychology. New York: Holt.

14. Kohl, H. 1995. *I won't learn from you.* New York: New Press.

15. Marcucci, O. February 2016. *The role of teacher buy-in in a restorative justice in a predominantly black school.* Paper presented at the Ethnography in Education Forum, Philadelphia, PA.

16. Breton, D. 2012. Decolonizing restorative justice *Tikkun,* Winter 2012: 45–47.

Chapter 7

1. https://nepc.colorado.edu/publication/restorative-justice

2. Reimer, K. E. 2020. Beyond order (Chapter 12). In *The School Leadership Survival Guide*. pp. 201–14.

   Blood, P., & M. Thorsborne. 2013. Understanding the change process. In *Implementing Restorative Practices in Schools: A Practical Guide to Transforming School Communities;* London: Jessica Kingsley Press.

   Vaandering, D., & D. Voelker. 2018. *Relationships First Implementation Guide: A Holistic, Whole School, Responsive Approach.* From: https://www. relationshipsfirstnl.com/_files/ugd/556f9d_1d363a4b-1d3846e096e2517f683261b2.pdf

3. Aquino, E. Manchester, H., & A. Wadhwa. 2021. *The Little Book of Youth Engagement in Restorative Justice.* Good Books.

4. For more information about monitoring and evaluation of rje implementation, we recommend the following resources:

   Brown, M. A. 2021. We cannot return to "normal": A post-COVID call for a systems approach to implementing restorative justice in education (rje).

   LAWS: Ambitions and Critiques of Restorative Justice (Special Edition), 10(68), https://doi.org/10.3390/laws10030068.

   Brown, M. A., & S. Di Lallo. 2020. Talking circles: A culturally responsive evaluation practice. *American Journal of Evaluation. 41*(3), 367–83 doi:10.1177/1098214019899164

   Thorsborne, M., N. Riestenberg & G. McCluskey. 2019. *Getting more out of restorative practice in schools: Practical approaches to improve school wellbeing and strengthen community engagement.* Jessica Kingsley Publishers.

About the Authors

Katherine Evans is an associate professor of education and restorative justice in education at Eastern Mennonite University in Virginia. Katherine helped develop EMU's graduate program in Restorative Justice in Education, which supports educators as they create more just and equitable educational opportunities for all students, including those marginalized based on race, ethnicity, income, ability, language, sexual orientation, and gender. She also serves as an education specialist with the Zehr Institute.

Dorothy Vaandering is a professor at the Faculty of Education at Memorial University in Newfoundland and Labrador. After an extensive career as a primary-elementary educator, she now researches the implementation and sustainability of restorative justice in education through critical theory and a decolonizing perspective. She works passionately to integrate restorative justice philosophy into theory and practice in her current role as researcher and teacher-educator. She is the director of the Relationships First: Restorative Justice in NL Research/Resource Centre, a center committed to developing relational communities of all kinds that honor Indigenous leadership and ways of being and knowing.